ARCHITECTURAL
STYLES A VISUAL GUIDE

ARCHITECTURAL

STYLES A VISUAL GUIDE

MARGARET FLETCHER
ILLUSTRATIONS BY ROBBIE POLLEY

CONTENTS

CHURCH OF ST LEOPOLD, Vienna, Austria

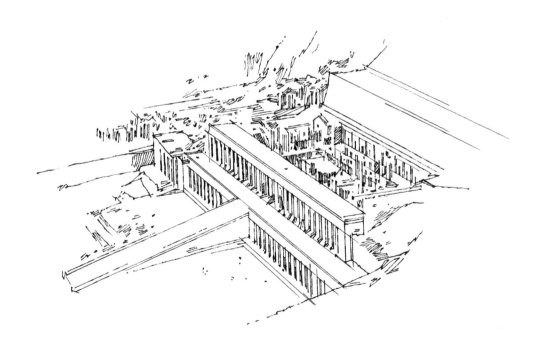

MORTUARY TEMPLE OF HATSHEPSUT, Deir el-Bahari, Egypt

INTRODUCTION

Architecture tells stories. Extant historic architecture allows us to reflect on and revel in the built environment of our ancestors, and to glimpse into their world. It connects us directly to our personal and collective past. Learning about architectural history allows us to travel back in time and understand more about previous cultures and civilizations, and discover what was important to their people. Was it religion? Self-expression? Cultural institutions? Urban or rural living? Wealth or family? One can stand in the footprints of Julius Caesar, Cleopatra, Shakespeare or any unknown individual, and begin to envision how life used to be.

Looking at architecture through all periods of time is important, not only because it formulates our basic understanding of the past, but also because it enriches our understanding of how each period influenced the next. Was it a progression, a rebellion or an outright rejection of what came before? It allows us to trace the evolution of the built environment, how architecture has changed over time, and how cross-cultural interactions have travelled across continents to spread knowledge. The relationship between

SANTA COSTANZA, Rome, Italy

architecture and culture is symbiotic: architecture impacts culture and society, and in turn culture and society impact architecture. The man-made heritage of architecture has shaped human experience, and continues to do so today.

This book organizes architecture by multiple means – time period, location, aesthetics, cultural and societal impact – all catalogued within a style. Defining architectural styles and the history of architecture has the luxury of reflection, although it should be noted that the idea of an architectural style is a relatively new concept. There is an abundance of stylistic and developmental overlap that occurs when looking at architecture over several thousand years. The very fact that we can categorize our built environment in this way reveals interesting inclinations that have developed over time. It is important to remember that style categories develop reflectively, so it is particularly challenging to discuss the development of architecture in contemporary times; this categorization has more to do with descriptive qualities than with an actual defined style because, for the moment, we lack time for reflection.

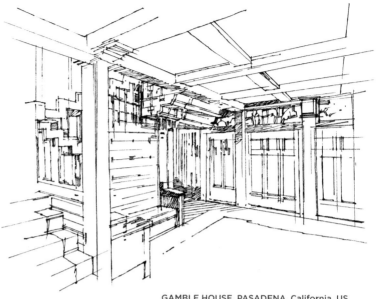

GAMBLE HOUSE, PASADENA, California, US

Contemporary architecture is moving at a rapid pace and its architects are often not keen to be labelled. They work within a set of objectives that are important both to the academy of architecture and to their individual clients; their work tends to fall into multiple categories and can be catalogued in a variety of ways. This book attempts to define the most compelling features of each piece of contemporary architecture, to encourage understanding of current practice. But remember, as style is a reflective process, and not the goal of a designer, these should be considered as rather fluid characterizations. At any given time in history, the people, the culture and the architects respond to the current situation. They act in the now, the present of that time.

This book, by design, is a visual narrative that will take you on a drawn journey through history. The illustrator, Robbie Polley, has created a masterful collection of architectural drawings that transcend photography and bring a warmth and human touch to the representation of the architectural examples. Each one is constructed with a careful hand and an eye for stylistic clarity. Humans are visual creatures; we understand

and remember things better if we see them. The drawings are therefore the primary feature to help you recognize associations between buildings within a certain style or period, as well as contrasts between different styles or periods. Each period discussed uses drawn examples to help you to assimilate visual elements and features, and begin to learn and identify the nature of each of the architectural styles in the buildings you may see day-to-day. Perhaps they will also inspire you to draw during your own architectural adventures!

The written descriptions aim to provide direct, clear and concise information for each example. While there are moments of specificity, the objective here is to give enough information to put each example within historic and stylistic context, and to present a broad visual and textual narrative of the history of architectural styles and design.

AD DEIR, Petra, Jordan

OKOCHI SANSO VILLA, Kyoto, Japan

The book is organized into five sections, four of which are focused on time-based architectural styles: Ancient and Classical, Medieval and Renaissance, Baroque to Art Nouveau, and Modern and Contemporary. Each of these sections is broken down into design styles and outlines the defining characteristics of each style. The final part of the book focuses on elements related to all styles of architecture – domes, columns, towers, arches and arcades, doorways, windows, pediments and gables, roofs, vaulting and stairways – each of which are represented with rich, drawn examples from multiple periods and styles.

This book is designed for architectural enthusiasts, history buffs, travellers, students or anyone who is curious about buildings and their environment. I hope it will enable you to journey through time and identify architectural features, classify buildings into specific architectural styles, recognize the relationships between periods and styles, understand the development of architectural elements, experience other cultures and places and consider the deep relationship we all share with the buildings we inhabit.

EMPIRE STATE BUILDING,
New York City, New York, US

TIMES SQUARE BUILDING,
Rochester, New York, US

THE
BUILDINGS

1

ANCIENT AND CLASSICAL

ANCIENT MIDDLE EAST

CIRCA 5300 BCE TO 650 CE

The primary building material of the Ancient Middle East was the mud brick. Typically consisting of mud, sand, loam, water and a binder such as straw, these bricks were either air-dried or fired in a kiln to increase their durability. Glazing techniques for bricks and tiles further increased durability and also allowed for additional ornamental advancements. The everyday homes of this era are no longer in existence, but what remain are the impressive ruins of palaces and temples associated with power and religion. Sculptors were highly skilled in depicting animal battles and grand beasts, surely intended to demonstrate the power of the kings. As such, relief-carved surfaces of brick became an important element of architectural decoration.

ANCIENT MIDDLE EAST
KEY FEATURES:

- **mud brick**
- **tile**
- **relief sculpture**
- **animal and human form in sculpture**
- **load-bearing construction**
- **ziggurat**

TAQ KASRA, Arch of Ctesiphon, Ctesiphon, Iraq, third to sixth centuries CE.

Built as part of an imperial complex, this is the largest brick catenary arch in the world. Constructed without a centring device or scaffolding, it was built by slanting the walls, brick layer by brick layer, until they met at the top.

ISHTAR GATE, Babylon, Iraq, 575 BCE.

Built as the main gate to the city of Babylon, the Ishtar Gate was dedicated to the Babylonian goddess Ishtar. It was part of a processional way over 0.8 km (0.5 miles) long with tall walls – 15 m (50 ft) – on each side. The gate itself is made with bricks, most of which are glazed in blue.

ZIGGURAT OF UR, Muqayyar, Iraq, twenty-first century BCE.

Oriented to true north, this stepped ziggurat has three levels of terraces, with three monumental staircases leading up to a gate on the first level. Constructed with large mud bricks, each level is supported by the one directly beneath. The temple at the top of the ziggurat did not survive, but the lower parts still exist and give evidence of construction and engineering methods.

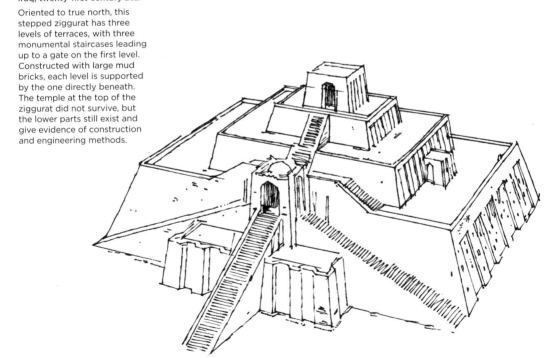

MUDHIF HOUSE, Iraq, circa 3300 BCE.

This typical Madan structure used for community gatherings is located in the swamps of southern Iraq and made from local reeds. The reeds were bundled into structural arches and arrayed across the space, with horizontal bundles acting as ties to the overall weaving of the exterior reed covering.

NAQSH-E ROSTAM NECROPOLIS, Fars Province, Iran, sixth to fourth centuries BCE.

The ancient necropolis is of the Achaemenid Dynasty and houses four tombs carved into caves high up on the stone cliffs. Only one of the tombs, for Darius the Great, is identifiable through an inscription.

TOMB OF DARIUS THE GREAT,
Naqsh-e Rostam, Iran, 485 BCE.

One of the four tombs of kings of the Achaemenid Empire, the monumental Tomb of Darius the Great is carved into a cliff. The tomb is in the shape of a cross, with an opening at the centre that leads to a small chamber where the king was buried.

PERSIAN COLUMN, Persepolis, Iran,
550–330 BCE.

This example of a Persian column is from the ancient city of Persepolis, the ceremonial capital of the Achaemenid Empire. The city had at least five palaces, and many of the structures were located upon a great plinth. This typical column capital was possibly part of the Apadana, a large hypostyle hall.

ANCIENT EGYPT

CIRCA 3000 TO 30 BCE

The buildings of Ancient Egypt were primarily associated with life, death and the celebration of the gods. The ruins of temples and tombs reveal that the architecture of Ancient Egypt did not follow a specific style, but rather used building practices of different types with associated features. The two most prominent building systems used were load-bearing and post-and-lintel structures. The load-bearing structures, built from uniform bricks and cut stone block, were massive in size and wall thickness, with sloping walls spreading wider at the base to support their weight and height. Post-and-lintel construction consisted of horizontal elements, in this case stone, bridging the gap between vertical members, columns. Columns were made of stacked stone, carved to shape, with capitals typically depicting abstracted forms of papyrus or lotus buds. The monumental buildings of Ancient Egypt were decorated with carved stone, hieroglyphics and paintings depicting elements expressing the power of gods, animals, humans and nature, as well as scenes of everyday life.

ANCIENT EGYPT KEY FEATURES:

- massive constructions
- monumental structures
- mud brick, limestone, sandstone, granite
- post-and-lintel construction
- load-bearing construction
- relief sculpture
- hieroglyphics

PYRAMID OF DJOSER, Saqqara Necropolis, Egypt, twenty-seventh century BCE, Imhotep, architect.

Originally covered in polished white limestone, the stepped pyramid is part of a large funereal complex and is the earliest pyramidal form in Egypt.

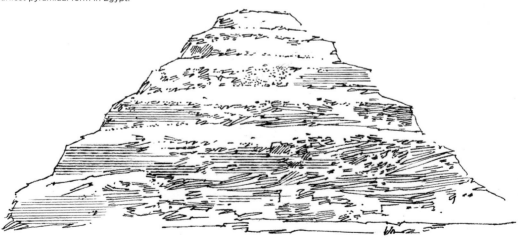

PYRAMID OF SNEFERU, Dahshur Necropolis, Egypt, 2600 BCE.

Called the Bent Pyramid because of the two different angles of inclination as the pyramid rises to its full height, it is believed that this particular pyramid was an experiment in construction and was found to be too steep during construction. It had to be adjusted to a shallower angle, thus the bend.

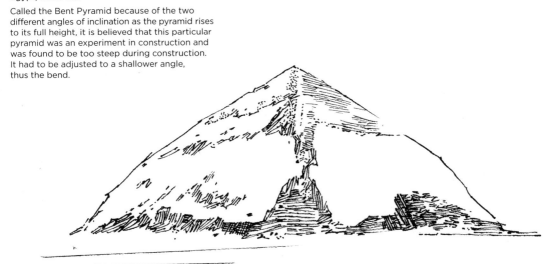

GIZA PYRAMID COMPLEX, Cairo, Egypt, 2560 BCE.

The Great Pyramid at Giza is the largest and oldest of the three pyramids at the Giza complex. Originally clad in limestone, the pyramid had a smooth white appearance. Intended as a tomb for Egyptian Pharaoh Khufu, there are three internal chambers currently detected within the structure.

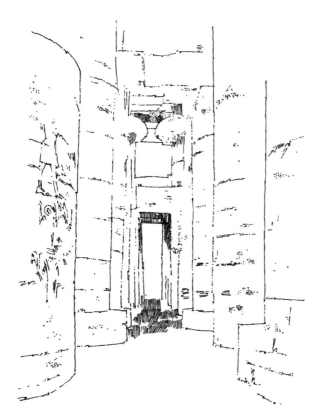

GREAT HYPOSTYLE HALL OF KARNAK TEMPLE COMPLEX, Karnak, Egypt, 2000–330 BCE.

This enormous structure covers around 5,000 sq m (6,000 sq yd) and has 134 columns in 16 rows. The temple is symmetrical, with ten larger columns flanking the central corridor and equal-sized wings on each side.

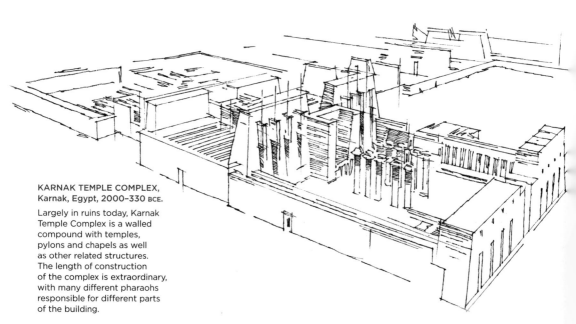

KARNAK TEMPLE COMPLEX, Karnak, Egypt, 2000–330 BCE.

Largely in ruins today, Karnak Temple Complex is a walled compound with temples, pylons and chapels as well as other related structures. The length of construction of the complex is extraordinary, with many different pharaohs responsible for different parts of the building.

ABU SIMBEL TEMPLES, Abu Simbel, Egypt, thirteenth century BCE.

The two temples at the Abu Simbel site are carved into sandstone cliffs at the edge of the River Nile. This, the entrance to the Small Temple, Temple of Hathor, was built by Ramesses II. The pylon-like facade has six colossal statues: figures of Ramesses, his wife Nefertari and their children.

TRAJAN'S KIOSK, Philae, Egypt, seventh century BCE.

Serving at one time as the main entrance to Philae, the structure now sits on the island of Agilkia – along with other important buildings of the Philae Temple Complex – to save it from the floodwaters of the River Nile after the installation of the Aswan High Dam. The fourteen column capitals have different plant forms and originally held a wood-frame roof.

COLONNADE, TEMPLE OF ISIS, Philae, Egypt, 690 BCE.

Two grand colonnades line the path towards the pylon at the entrance to the Temple of Isis at Philae. All the column capitals are plant-like, yet no two are alike.

PILLARS OF THE MAMMISI CHAPEL, Temple of Isis, Philae, Egypt, seventh century BCE.

A mammisi is a small chapel attached to a larger temple, in this case the Temple of Isis at Philae. Also known as a birth house, this type of temple was used for the annual ceremony to honour the birth of the child of the god to which it was dedicated. The column capitals shown here have animal heads resting on top of plant forms.

TEMPLE OF HORUS, Edfu, Egypt, 57 BCE.

Buried under hundreds of years of sand,
excavation of the temple began in the mid-
nineteenth century. This view of the first pylon
and main entrance to the temple shows the
monumental mass of the load-bearing structure.
The base of the pylon is considerably thicker than
the top, necessary to support the overall weight
and height. Typically, these pylons were decorated
with carved scenes proclaiming the power and
authority of the pharaoh.

PRE-COLUMBIAN

1500 BCE TO 1532 CE

The Pre-Columbian era is recognized for its complex civilizations incorporating an agricultural lifestyle within an urban structure of social class. The builders of this time were known for their advanced understanding of astronomy and engineering, and built their cities aligned with astronomical and natural features. Typically, buildings were constructed of mud brick and stone. The stone was often a native volcanic rock that was soft enough to allow for intricate carvings, such that many of the buildings were decorated with images of cultural and religious importance. Pre-Columbian architecture flourished in the Mesoamerican region, containing parts of Mexico and Central America. Entire cities with pyramids, temples, platforms, open squares, ball courts and sacrificial altars were indicative of the grand civilizations of this period.

PRE-COLUMBIAN KEY FEATURES:

- monolithic structures
- mud brick
- carved stone
- rectilinear and trapezoidal apertures
- load-bearing construction
- urban civilizations
- astronomical alignments
- ceremonial buildings

TEMPLE OF THE INSCRIPTIONS, Palenque, Mexico, 700 CE, Maya.

Built as a funerary monument for K'inich Janaab' Pakal, the complex consists of a temple atop an eight-stepped pyramid with a central stair. Originally the monument would have been covered in stucco and painted red. The temple is named after the three hieroglyphic tablets found on the walls inside.

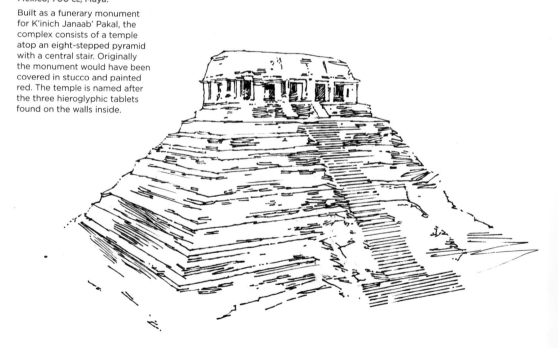

CEMPOALA STONE RING, Úrsulo Galván Municipality, Veracruz, Mexico, 900–1168 CE, Toltec, a contemporary civilization of Aztec.

Part of a larger complex of temples, a palace and several mounds, there are three stone rings of varying sizes. The rings are made from beach stones stacked together to make small pillars, and are thought to support the understanding of astronomical cycles.

ANCIENT CITY OF COPÁN, Copán, Honduras, 250–900 CE, Maya.

This sculpture is found on the ruins at the ancient city of Copán. The site includes stone temples, two pyramids, plazas, stairways and a ball court, all elevated on a plinth. Common subjects of Maya art are royalty and celestial beings, often worked in limestone and volcanic tuff.

TEMPLE II, Tikal, Guatemala, 200–900 CE, Maya.

There are many ancient buildings at Tikal, including six large temples. Temple II was a funerary temple for the wife of Jasaw Chan K'awiil. The temple rises up a monumental stairway to a summit shrine with a carving of the queen on the main lintel over the doorway.

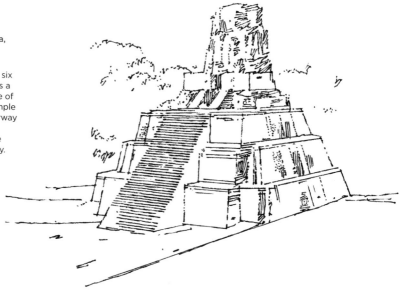

EL CARACOL OBSERVATORY TEMPLE, Chichen Itza, Tinúm Municipality, Yucatán State, Mexico, circa 600–850 CE, Maya.

The spiral staircase inside the tower of this structure led to the name El Caracol, which means snail in Spanish. Used as an observatory, the tower is raised on a platform, affording clear views, and is thought to be in particular alignment to Venus, an important planet for the Maya people.

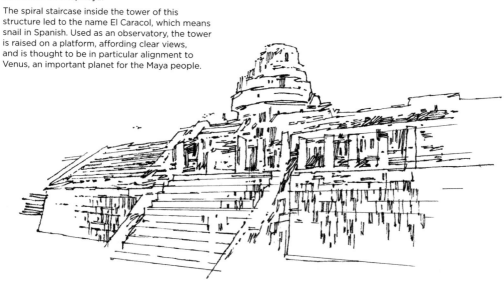

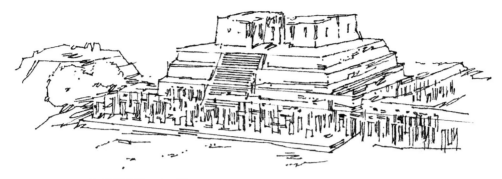

TEMPLO DE LOS GUERREROS (Temple of the Warriors), Chichen Itza, Tinúm Municipality, Yucatán State, Mexico, 1200 CE, Maya.

One of the best-preserved temples at Chichen Itza, it consists of a large stepped pyramid surrounded by row upon row of columns representing warriors. Officially part of the Group of the Thousand Columns, they supported a large wood or thatch roof structure that housed religious or civic events.

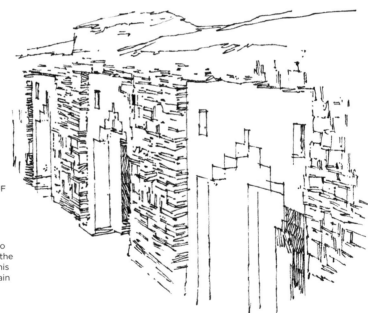

TEMPLE OF THE VIRGINS OF THE SUN, Isla de la Luna, Lake Titicaca, Bolivia, 1000–1500 CE, Inca.

Thought to be a residential complex for Inca women who were either noble or part of the aristocracy, the remains of this temple open onto a large plain overlooking Lake Titicaca.

MACHU PICCHU, near Cusco, Peru, 1450–1532 CE, Inca.

Perched high in the Andes Mountains, this Inca city is considered a royal estate, which housed about 750 workers in support of the holdings. The siting of the city and its important buildings relates to views towards sacred mountains (*apas*), and cardinal orientation. Buildings were made of stone with no mortar set between them and wedged together tightly, providing flexibility and stability in an area rife with seismic activity. Farming was done on the surrounding man-made terraces on the mountain side.

A typical house in the tightly packed residential district of Machu Picchu. The structures were made from stones fitted together with no mortar, a technique called ashlar, and had wooden, straw-thatched roofs.

TEMPLE OF THE FEATHERED SERPENT,
Xochicalco, Mexico, 900 CE, Aztec.

This structure is significant because of the carved depiction of eight enormous serpents with feather flourishes on their heads. The intricate carvings surrounding the serpents are thought to describe a calling together of leaders of the Mesoamerican calendar called 'The Lords of Time'. The temple consists of a base of the talud-tablero form, with the talud, inward-sloping walls, and the tablero, the protruding top tier that extends over the edge of the sloping wall, much like a tabletop.

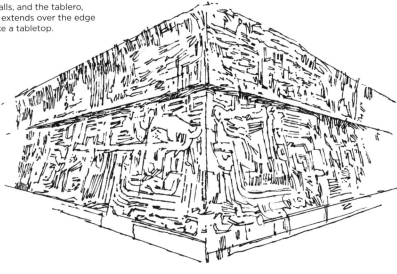

SANTA CECILIA ACATITLAN, Tlalnepantla de Baz, near Mexico City, Mexico, 900–1521 CE, Aztec.

Partially destroyed during the Spanish Conquest (1519–21), the pyramid was reconstructed in the 1960s amid some controversy around appropriate alterations. Thought to be dedicated to Huitzilopochtli and Tlaloc, the building has one large staircase to the temple at the top.

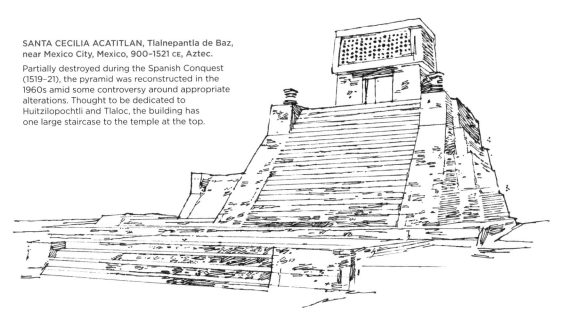

PRE-CLASSICAL
1600 TO 100 BCE

The Pre-Classical era of architecture encompasses the work of the Mycenean and Etruscan cultures. Mycenean architecture is that of the Mycenean people that dominated Greece from about 1600 to 1200 BCE, primarily consisting of citadels – walled enclosures housing the palace and homes of important societal figures – and tombs. The most spectacular of these tombs were underground beehive constructions intended for kings; the more common rock-cut tombs were for the general population.

Just as Mycenean architecture can be seen as a precursor to Ancient Greek, Etruscan architecture (eighth to second century BCE) is considered a forerunner of Ancient Roman. The architectural work of the Etruscans reached a pinnacle with the development of a specific temple type inspired by the Greeks. Typically located in the centre of a town, the temples were initially made of mud and brick, but over time this mighty engineering culture developed methods to construct them from stone.

PRE-CLASSICAL KEY FEATURES:

- monumental gateways
- citadel construction
- beehive tombs
- mud brick
- stone
- temple development

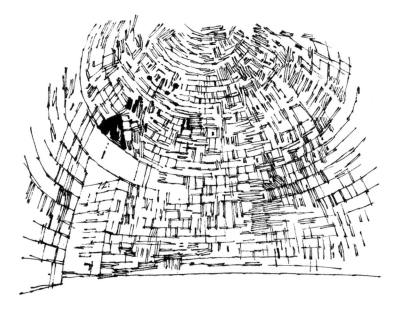

TREASURY OF ATREUS, Mycenae, Greece, 1250 BCE.

The Tomb of Agamemnon is a simple yet monumental structure of a corbelled dome excavated into a hill. It is approached via a long, walled path and through a grand entrance with an enormous stone lintel bridging the opening. Once inside, the construction of the large tholos, or beehive tomb, becomes evident as the stone work is fully visible.

The open triangle above the lintel, called a relieving triangle, is placed to distribute the weight above the lintel to prevent it from collapsing.

NECROPOLIS OF BANDITACCIA, Cerveteri,
Italy, ninth to third centuries BCE.

As the site of a large, ancient Etruscan city, it is
thought the population of Cerveteri could have
been as many as 30,000. The Necropolis of
Banditaccia contains thousands of Etruscan-era
tombs, ranging from rectilinear tombs arranged
on parallel streets, to those in an adjacent area
mostly housed in circular tumuli.

CITADEL OF MYCENAE, Argolis, Greece,
1350–1200 BCE.

Considered the most important area of civilization
of the period, this fortified city, located between
the Aegean and mainland Greece, was positioned
to control commerce in the area. The walls of
the citadel were cyclopean: constructed of large
limestone boulders with smaller bits of limestone
to fill the gaps. The term was initiated by the
Greeks, who thought that the only way the stones
could have been lifted into place was if the giant
Cyclops had moved them himself.

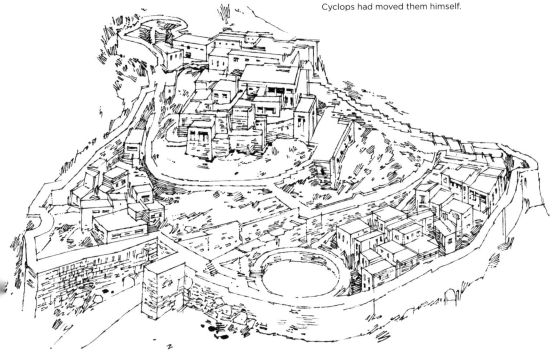

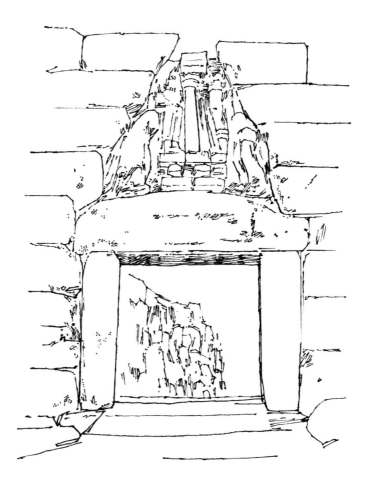

LION GATE, Mycenae, Greece, 1250 BCE.

This gate is the primary entrance to the fortified citadel of
Mycenae. The relief sculpture of two lions is one of the few
surviving sculptures of this time. The gate consists of two
monolithic vertical members with a large lintel stretching
across the opening and resting on the vertical stones. It is
presumed that there was a wooden door spanning the
3-m (10-ft) opening, providing controlled entry to the city.

PORTONACCIO TEMPLE, Veii, Italy, circa 510 BCE.

Understood largely through ruins and
reconstructions, monumental temples to
worship gods began to emerge in Etruscan
culture around 600 BCE, possibly through the
influence of Greek architecture. The temples
were made from stone foundations with colourful
wood, mud brick and terracotta structures.
Tuscan columns were developed at this time
and were essentially Doric columns with a base.
The greatest resource on Etruscan architecture
was published in *De architectura* by Vitruvius.

Etruscan temples were
decorated with terracotta
statues of larger-than-life
figures, called acroteria, on
the roof peaks and edges. This
example from the Portonaccio
Temple is likely an antefix, a
vertical ornament that caps the
end of a row of roof tiles, and
depicts the form of a maenad,
a female follower of Bacchus.

ANCIENT GREEK
CIRCA 900 BCE TO 100 CE

The temple form was the architectural stalwart following the decline of the Mycenean culture. As one of the most important public buildings, the temple developed over time and had a variety of configurations, but the use of the peristyle – a row of encompassing columns around the building – remained a true and unique feature of the Greek temple. Along with the peristyle, other typical elements included the portico, pronaos, naos and opisthodomos – the rear porch.

Systems of proportion were extremely important in Greek architecture to achieve balance and symmetry, and all elements existed in harmonious relationship. Along with the temple, most prominent Greek towns also included an open-air theatre – usually sited on a hill with a half-circle of tiered seats; a palaestra – a gymnasium for male citizens; and perhaps a hippodrome for horse racing.

ANCIENT GREEK KEY FEATURES:
- intricate detail
- tall columns
- symmetry
- harmony
- Doric, Ionic and Corinthian orders
- temple architecture
- post-and-lintel construction

PARTHENON, Athens, Greece, 447–432 BCE, Iktinos and Kallikrates, architects.

This colossal temple, dedicated to the goddess Athena, stands at the crest of the Acropolis. It is a peripteral building, meaning it is framed by a pedimented portico with columns on all four sides of the post-and-lintel structure. The inner cella, enclosed room, is divided into two spaces and surrounded by columns supporting a low-relief Ionic frieze. The row of columns surrounding the temple are Doric and have entasis, a slight convex curve in the column shaft, applied to mitigate the optical illusion of straight columns appearing cinched in at the middle. The columns also lean in and are larger at the corners where the spacing between them is slightly reduced. The stylobate – stepped pedestal – is slightly domed and droops gracefully downwards as does the entablature. Several theories abound – some say the doming was designed to remove rainwater from the structure; others claim the illusions were designed to offset the natural visual bending of such a long, straight structure; and others postulate the architects wanted to animate the static nature of all of the straight lines through curves.

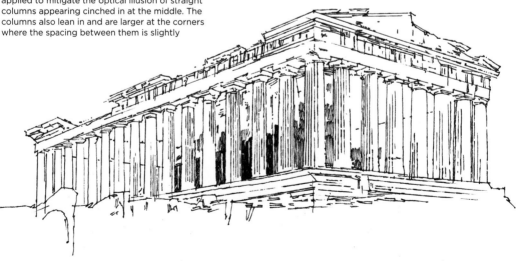

ERECHTHEION, Athens, Greece, 406 BCE, Mnesikles, thought to be architect.

This Ancient Greek temple is located on the north side of the Acropolis and is known for the caryatids, six female forms acting as supporting columns that surround the south porch of the temple.

TEMPLE OF HEPHAESTUS, Athens, Greece, 450–415 BCE.

As one of the best-preserved temples in Greece, it is a fantastic example of a Doric peripteral building. In the centre of the temple lies a cella and an entrance room called the pronaos, as well as an opisthodomos, a rear room of the temple on axis with the cella and pronaos but only opening to the rear portico and not the inner cella.

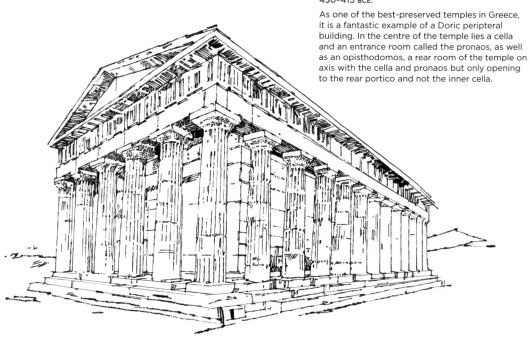

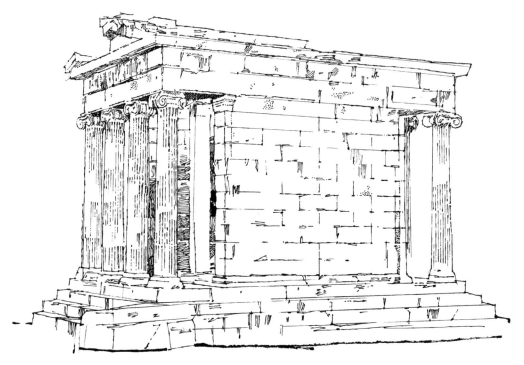

TEMPLE OF ATHENA NIKE, Athens, Greece, 420 BCE, Kallikrates, architect.

This temple is smaller than others on the Acropolis, with columns on the back and front but not the sides of the cella. Built in the Ionic order in white Pentelic marble, the columns are entirely monolithic in that they are carved from one piece of stone rather than a series of stacked, carved drums.

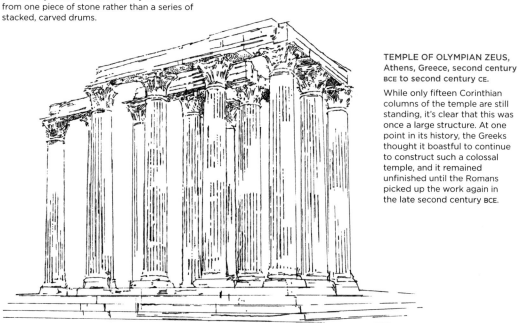

TEMPLE OF OLYMPIAN ZEUS, Athens, Greece, second century BCE to second century CE.

While only fifteen Corinthian columns of the temple are still standing, it's clear that this was once a large structure. At one point in its history, the Greeks thought it boastful to continue to construct such a colossal temple, and it remained unfinished until the Romans picked up the work again in the late second century BCE.

CHORAGIC MONUMENT OF LYSICRATES, Athens, Greece, circa 335 BCE.

Noted as the first use of Corinthian order on the exterior of a structure, the monument stands on a tall rectangular podium and is one of the few surviving choragic monuments, defined as a freestanding pedestal for a choral or theatrical prize.

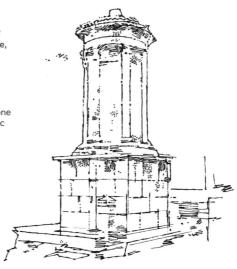

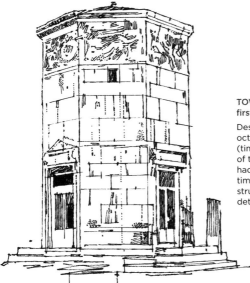

TOWER OF THE WINDS, Athens, Greece, first or second century BCE.

Designed as a device to measure time, the octagonal structure, also known as a horologion (timepiece), is built of Pentelic marble. Each side of the building faces a point of the compass and had a vertical sundial under the frieze to cast a time-telling shadow on each face. Originally the structure had a bronze weather vane on top to determine wind direction.

FRIEZE OF THE SIPHNIAN TREASURY, Delphi, Greece, circa 525 BCE.

This sculpted frieze depicts a lion attacking Apollo and is from the north side of the Siphnian Treasury. This type of scene is a Gigantomachy, depicting a battle between animals and the Olympian gods. The treasury was almost fully enclosed, with a front porch and pediment supported by two columns in the form of maidens set between pilasters at either edge of the porch.

ANCIENT ROMAN
753 BCE TO 476 CE

The Roman Empire looked to both the Greek and Etruscan civilizations for Classical architectural elements. However, there were some significant differences that led to the adaptation and advancement of architecture during this period. Greek towns were typically organized through symbolic ideals, whereas Roman towns were largely laid out according to military principles and objectives. The Roman way of life and vast nature of the empire necessitated a larger range of building types, and the development of the arch, vault and dome radically altered the possibilities of construction. In addition, engineering advances in the available materials – tufa, marble, concrete and the development of fired brick leading to brick-faced concrete – combined with the desire for larger, more monumental structures progressed Roman architecture.

The Romans also faced additional engineering challenges such as the movement of water and food across long distances to support the growth of the empire in regions that lacked natural resources, thus the development of the aqueduct and durable road systems. There was also a much freer application of the orders – Doric, Ionic, Corinthian, and later with the development of Tuscan and Composite – than was ever permitted through the symbology of Greek ideals.

ANCIENT ROMAN KEY FEATURES:

- arches
- vaults
- domes
- concrete
- large public buildings
- aqueducts
- urban planning
- monumental structures
- Tuscan and Composite orders

(Opposite) PANTHEON, Rome, Italy, 113–125 CE.

As the best-preserved Ancient Roman monument, the Pantheon, once a pagan temple, is now a Catholic Church, the Basilica di Santa Maria ad Martyres. The main building is cylindrical with an attached pedimented portico with sixteen Corinthian columns. The interior boasts a spectacular coffered concrete dome with an open oculus at the apex. The diameter of the rotunda is the exact same measurement as the maximum height of the dome.

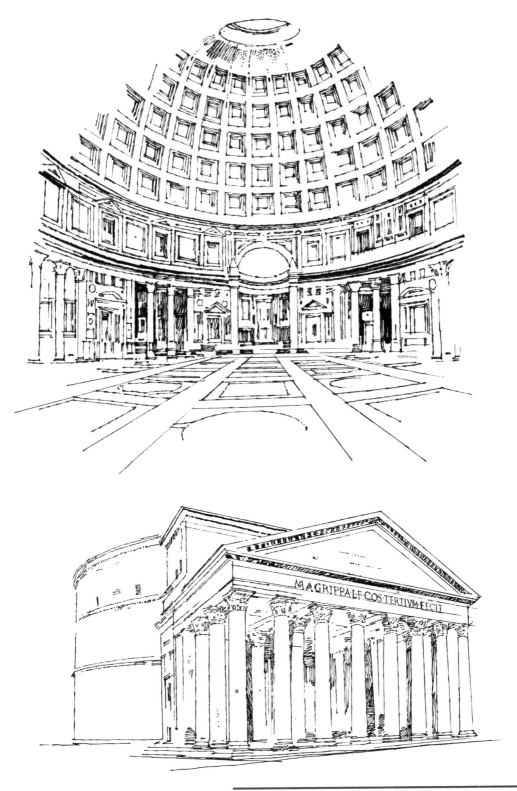

TEMPLE OF PORTUNUS, Rome, Italy, late second or early first century BCE.

Constructed of travertine, tufa and stucco, this small temple is built in the Ionic order. It is a rectangular form with freestanding columns on the front porch supporting the pediment above. The remaining columns surrounding the temple are engaged columns attached to the other three faces of the temple structure.

ROMAN FORUM, Rome, Italy, 500 BCE.

The Roman Forum is now a large open plaza in the centre of Rome, with multiple ruins, most of which were government buildings. The Forum was the centre of activity for the city, with structures dedicated to religion, social events, sport, law and military processions. In this view, the Temple of Saturn can be seen in the foreground with the Arch of Septimius Severus in the centre. Santi Luca e Martina can be seen in the rear.

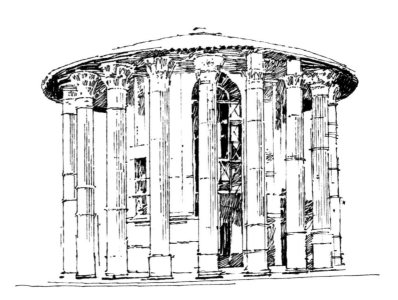

TEMPLE OF HERCULES VICTOR, Rome, Italy, second century BCE, Hermodoros of Salamina, architect.

Built of Greek marble, this temple in the round is encircled by twenty Corinthian columns. The original architrave and roof are gone, replaced with a tiled roof. Considered the earliest surviving marble temple in Rome, it is thought to have been constructed by Greek architect Hermodoros of Salamina, who was working in Rome during this period.

COLOSSEUM, Rome, Italy, 70–80 CE.

This colossal amphitheatre could seat upwards of 50,000 spectators. It was quite different from previous amphitheatres in that it was freestanding and not embedded in a hillside. Constructed of stone and concrete, the circular structure has three storeys of arcades, each with a different order of engaged column: Doric, Ionic and Corinthian. Gruesome contests between men and animals or duelling gladiators took place for the entertainment of the Romans.

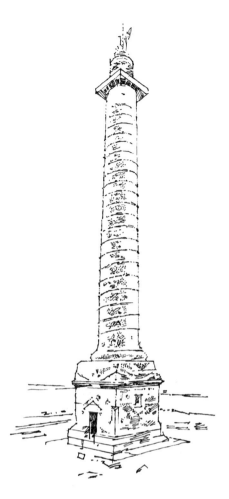

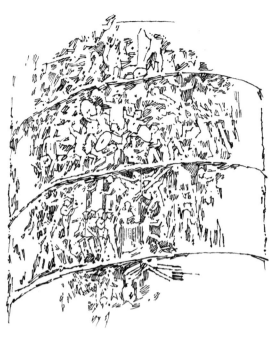

TRAJAN'S COLUMN, Rome, Italy, 113 CE, Apollodorus of Damascus, architect.

This monumental column, designed as a war memorial for the Roman Emperor Trajan, stands 38 m (125 ft) tall and was constructed using nineteen drums of marble. Low-relief carvings on the shaft spiral around the column with a 200-m-long (656 ft) narrative of Trajan's successful battles in Dacia, modern-day Romania. Originally there were viewing structures on each side from which you could admire the sculpted surface. Upon his death, Trajan's remains were buried within the foundation.

TEMPLE OF HERCULES, Cori, Italy, 89–80 BCE.

Once an important and active region located 45 km (28 miles) southeast of Rome, the town of Cori lost much of its relevance when the Appian Way was constructed 10 km (6 miles) away and virtually bypassed the town. This Doric temple with clear Hellenistic influences sits atop the town's acropolis.

TEMPLE OF BACCHUS, Baalbek, Lebanon,
late second or early third century CE.

Resting on a podium, the temple boasts
forty-two Corinthian columns arranged
around the periphery. The interior of the cella
is richly adorned with engaged Corinthian
columns on a wall with two levels of carved
niches. This temple has some of the most
abundant and skilful sculpture and relief
carving to exist from ancient times.

PORTA NIGRA, Trier, Germany, 170 CE.

This large Roman city gate was originally built in
grey sandstone and flanked by two semicircular
towers. It was one of four gates that led into the
fortified city. The gate has seen many uses over
the years: it served as a home for the monk
Simeon during the eleventh century, and then
as a church until Napoleon dissolved the Church
and restored it to its ancient purpose in the early
nineteenth century.

PONT DU GARD, Nimes, France, circa first century CE.

Spanning the River Gardon, this marvel of Roman engineering was designed to carry water to the city of Nimes. With three tiers of arches, and with the largest arched spans at the lower level, the aqueduct was built without mortar, true to typical large Roman constructions.

CASTEL SANT'ANGELO, Rome, Italy, 123–39 CE.

Built in the second century as a mausoleum for Roman Emperor Hadrian, the structure was converted into a fortress during the fifth century. The form is a circle inscribed within a square with projecting barbicans designed for defensive measures. During the fourteenth century, the papacy converted the fortress into a castle and connected it to St Peter's Basilica by an elevated and fortified corridor.

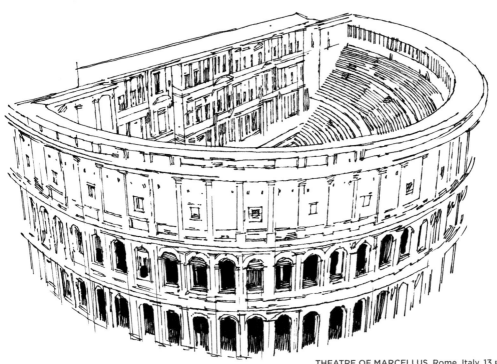

THEATRE OF MARCELLUS, Rome, Italy, 13 BCE.

This reconstruction demonstrates the structure's obvious influence on the facade of the Colosseum. Begun by Julius Caesar, the construction required the demolition of the ancient Flaminian Circus as well as the slight moving of the Temple of Apollo Sosianus. The semicircular facade was made of travertine and has two tiers of arches: engaged Doric columns on the lower tier and engaged Ionic columns on the second.

ARCH OF CONSTANTINE, Rome, Italy, 315 CE.

Commemorating the victory of Roman Emperor Constantine over Maxentius at the Battle of Milvian Bridge in Rome, this is the largest existing Roman triumphal arch. Constructed of Proconnesian marble, the monument has three identically proportioned arches: a large one at the centre flanked by two smaller at either side. Four Corinthian columns with a statue on top face each side of the monument. Multiple colours of marble were used in the carved elements, giving the monument a striking appearance.

EARLY AND CLASSICAL CHINA
1500 BCE TO NINETEENTH CENTURY CE

Chinese architecture has, at its roots, core values that permeate all structures, though they vary aesthetically across regions. In 1103, Li Jie wrote a treatise on the architecture of China called *Yingzao Fashi – Treatise on Architectural Methods* – in an effort to record historic examples of traditional architecture as well as codify a set of ideals to be followed to gain a consistency of style. Topics covered ranged from structural directives such as building without a foundation and using wood mortise and tenon joints to protect structures during earthquakes, to more aesthetic ideals related to colour systems for building elements.

EARLY AND CLASSICAL CHINA KEY FEATURES:

- heavy timber construction
- mortise and tenon construction
- curved and upturned roof lines
- rooftop statuary
- lion statues at temple and palace entrances
- glazed roof tiles
- system of bright colours

HUMBLE ADMINISTRATOR'S GARDEN, Suzhou, China, twelfth century CE.

This small pavilion – the Secluded Pavilion of the Phoenix Tree and Bamboo – is set within this classical Jiangnan garden that is organized in three parts around a lake. Buildings, ponds, paths, bridges and landscape are specifically arranged for peaceful passage and tranquil views. The pavilion is located in the central garden and is noted for its circular entryways, which provide multi-layered views framed through the visually overlapping circles.

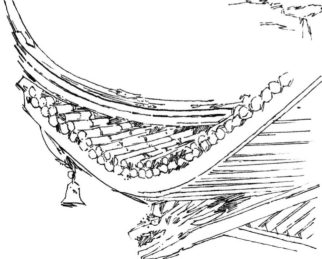

The upturned and curved corners of Chinese roofs are one of their clearest identifying features. This example is possibly from the south, where the steepness of the curve aided in the drainage of rainwater. Wide eaves protected the wooden walls and brackets below from water damage, while rows of cupped interlocking roof tiles also helped with water drainage and provided some protection from fire. Bells were often hung at roof corners and provided a harmonious sound while warding off evil spirits.

TEMPLE OF HEAVEN, Beijing, China 1406–1420 CE.

This triple-gabled circular building, built on three levels of tiered white marble, is the Hall of Prayer for Good Harvests and the largest of the three main buildings in the Temple of Heaven compound. There is some elegant symbolism at play in the design of the temple grounds: earth is represented by a square and heaven by a circle. This geometric relationship is repeated through all the structures housed there, reinforcing the symbolic relationship.

PAVILION OF PRINCE TENG, Nanchang, Jiangxi, China, 653 CE.

Destroyed and rebuilt twenty-nine times, this pavilion, one of the most significant of the Tang Dynasty, served as an imperial structure where scholars met to write and discuss issues of cultural importance. Considered one of the Three Great Towers of Jiangnan, it sits with prominence as an infrequently found piece of royal architecture in southern China.

SAKYAMUNI PAGODA, Fogong Temple, Shanxi, China, 1056 CE.

This is one of the oldest and tallest wood-structured pagodas in China. Built on a tall stone platform, the octagonal building has nine interior levels, though only five are visible from the exterior; between each visible roof is an intermediary level evident by an exterior balcony. Known for its bracket arm construction (dougong brackets), it features fifty-four different bracket forms. There are Buddha statues on three of the interior levels.

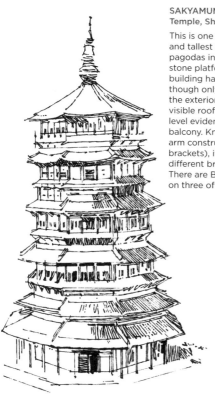

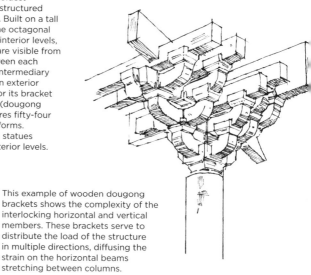

This example of wooden dougong brackets shows the complexity of the interlocking horizontal and vertical members. These brackets serve to distribute the load of the structure in multiple directions, diffusing the strain on the horizontal beams stretching between columns.

FORBIDDEN CITY, Beijing, China, 1406–1420 CE.

This building, the Gate of Divine Might, is one of four gates surrounding the Forbidden City, a walled imperial palace complex in the heart of Beijing. The four gates are the Meridian Gate (main entry), the Gate of Divine Might (main exit), East Glorious Gate and West Glorious Gate. Each gate faces a different cardinal orientation and sits within the massive, 8-m-tall (26 ft) defensive walls constructed of rammed earth and surrounded by a 52-m-wide (171 ft) and 6 m (20 ft) deep moat.

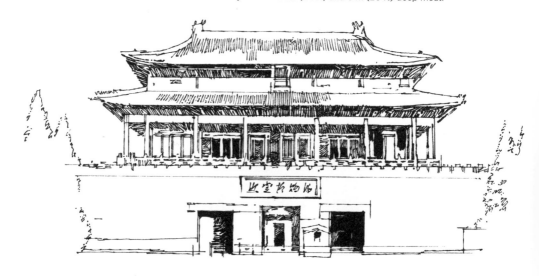

TOWER OF BUDDHIST INCENSE, Summer Palace, Beijing, China, 1764 CE.

Originally intended to be a nine-storey religious structure, this was dismantled and redesigned as a Buddhist tower during construction. It has three levels and is octagonal in shape. Inside is a gilded statue of Guanyin, a bodhisattva associated with compassion. A bodhisattva is a person on the path toward awakening in Buddhism, who spends their life assisting and saving others.

POTALA PALACE, Lhasa, Tibet, China, 1645 CE.

This enormous administrative and religious complex rises up from the hillside and is considered a significant pilgrimage site for Tibetan Buddhists. A protected fortress due to its elevated and inclusive construction, the palace was the winter residence of the Dalai Lamas until the mid-twentieth century. With thick walls built of rammed earth and stone, it has over one thousand rooms.

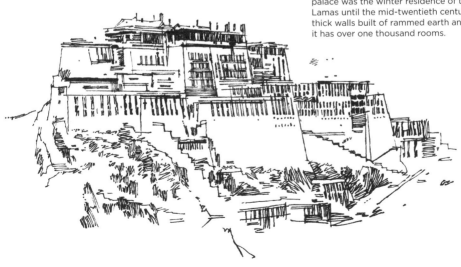

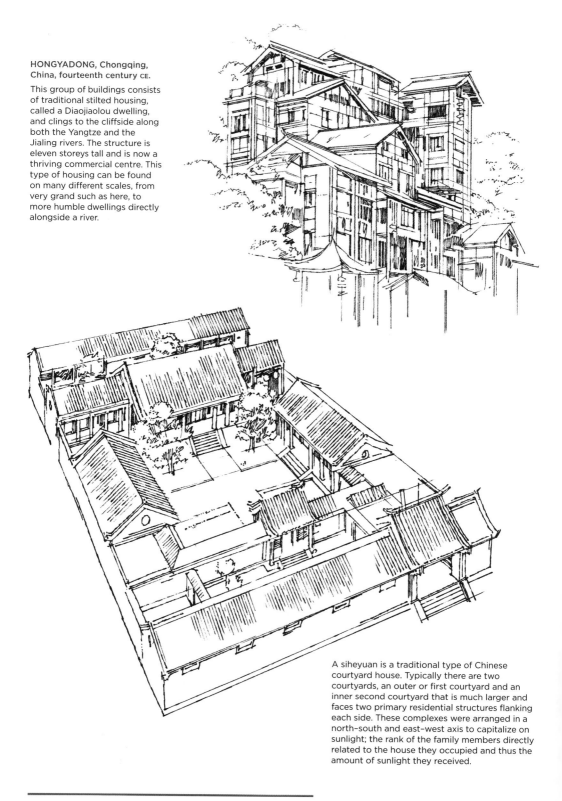

HONGYADONG, Chongqing, China, fourteenth century CE.

This group of buildings consists of traditional stilted housing, called a Diaojiaolou dwelling, and clings to the cliffside along both the Yangtze and the Jialing rivers. The structure is eleven storeys tall and is now a thriving commercial centre. This type of housing can be found on many different scales, from very grand such as here, to more humble dwellings directly alongside a river.

A siheyuan is a traditional type of Chinese courtyard house. Typically there are two courtyards, an outer or first courtyard and an inner second courtyard that is much larger and faces two primary residential structures flanking each side. These complexes were arranged in a north–south and east–west axis to capitalize on sunlight; the rank of the family members directly related to the house they occupied and thus the amount of sunlight they received.

HANGING TEMPLE, Datong, China, 491 CE.

Hanging from the cliffside of Hengshan Mountain, this temple is thought to have been built by one person, a monk named Liao Ran. The location protects it against flood waters and the ravages of mountain rain and snow. The monastery is devoted to three religious practices – Buddhism, Taoism and Confucianism – and has six main halls and thirty-four less significant halls connected through passageways and bridges. The engineering of the temple relies on wooden pillars and girders anchored into the rock.

SONGYUE PAGODA, Dengfeng, China, 523 CE.

The pagoda, originally built as a seasonal palace for Emperors Xuanwu and Xiaoming, was converted to a Buddhist temple in the late sixth century. It is the oldest brick pagoda in existence and the only structure remaining from the temple grounds. It is a dodecagon – twelve-sided – with fifteen outer layers and ten inner layers. The exterior of the pagoda shapes a smooth parabolic curve as the floors reach the apex, and is thought to have been influenced in form by Indian Buddhist structures.

EARLY AND CLASSICAL JAPAN
PRE-SIXTH CENTURY BCE TO NINETEENTH CENTURY CE

Before Buddhism arrived in the sixth century, the primary religion of early Japan was Shintoism, based on the premise that spiritual powers exist in the natural world. These spirits, called kami, live in natural places, such as animals, plants, mountains and rivers. Shinto architecture is centred on the shrine – with an inner hall that only priests can enter – and marked by a special gateway called a torii, which establishes the demarcation between the sacred area of the shrine and the outside world. When Buddhism arrived with influences from China and Korea, architectural elaboration increased. Buddhist temples typically have ornamental brackets under the roof, decorative columns, bright painted colours, carved surfaces and gilding in silver and gold.

EARLY AND CLASSICAL JAPAN
KEY FEATURES:

- delicate
- harmonious
- elaborate joinery
- torii gates
- Shinto shrines
- Buddhist temples

YOMEIMON GATE, Toshogu Shrine, Nikko, Japan, 1617 CE.

Covered with over five hundred carvings depicting traditional scenes of everyday life, this two-storey gate is one of the fifty-five structures found at this Shinto shrine. The carvings are richly painted and of deep relief. The elaborate nature of the gate demonstrates the status of the family responsible for its construction.

FUSHIMI INARI, Kyoto, Japan, 711 CE.

This Shinto shrine is famous for the thousands of red torii gates that follow multiple trails up into the forest of sacred Mount Inari. This giant torii in front of the Romon Gate marks the entrance to the shrine grounds: the division between the secular world and the sacred world of the Shinto shrine. The gates are typically made of wood, with two vertical posts and two horizontal members spanning the opening.

The Romon, or main gate, marks the procession from the monumental torii gate up a large stair to the main entrance to the shrine. The stairs are flanked by sculptures of foxes, thought to be messengers of Inari, the Shinto god of rice, sake, merchants and manufacturers.

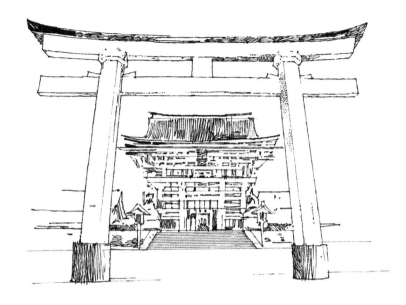

PHOENIX HALL, Byodoin Temple, Kyoto, Japan, 1053 CE.

Phoenix Hall is the main temple building of the Byodoin monastery. There is a central building housing the Amida Buddha, with twin L-shaped open-air corridors on each side. The Amida was sculpted by Jocho using multiple layers of wood in a technique called yosegi. Upon the clay-tiled roof are two phoenix sculptures, one on each end of the ridge.

HORYU-JI TEMPLE, Nara, Japan, 607 CE.

Horyu-ji is a Buddhist temple that has served as a monastery and a seminary. The two-storey Kondo, main hall, seen here, is one of the oldest wooden buildings in the world. The irimoya roof is a tiled hip and gable roof. The compound features architectural elements typical of the period: columns with entasis, double-terraced platforms to ground the structures, inverted V-shaped support posts and columns topped with wooden brackets to disperse the heavy load of the tiled roof.

MATSUMOTO CASTLE KEEP, Matsumoto, Japan, sixteenth century CE.

The keep is made of wood and stone and perched on a flat plain surrounded by a moat; the entire structure is classified as a flatland castle. With thin windows, sama, on the upper levels for firing arrows, and an observation deck on the sixth (top) floor, as well as openings through which to drop stones onto enemies, the keep was set up as the last defence of the castle grounds.

TRADITIONAL JAPANESE TOWNHOUSE
(Machiya), Japan, seventeenth to nineteenth
centuries CE.

The existing machiya in Kyoto provide a
fundamental view into the architectural character
of urban neighbourhoods. Long and narrow, these
homes reach far into the urban block and often
have one or two interior courtyards. The front
of the home was reserved for business activities,
while the primary residential area was near the
back. The pattern of wood lattice at the front of
the home described the nature of the business
found within.

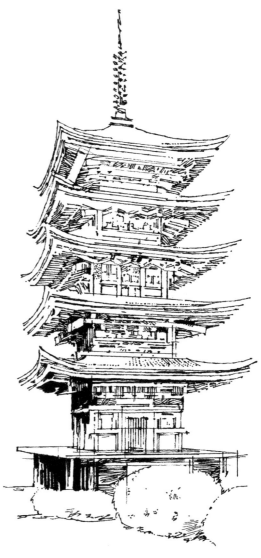

RURIKO-JI PAGODA,
Yamaguchi, Japan, 1442 CE.

One of the three most revered
pagodas in Japan, this
five-storey building is part of
the Buddhist temple complex
and pre-dates the main temple.
It is hollow inside, with five
overlapping wooden sections,
one for each level, as the
pagoda rises. Inside is a central
pillar called a shinbashira, that
is anchored to the ground but
only touches the finial at the
apex of the tower, allowing it
to shift and bend during any
seismic activity.

INUYAMA CASTLE, Inuyama, Japan, 1537 CE.

Recognized as the smallest and oldest of the twelve original castles still existing in Japan, Inuyama Castle is perched on top of a hill adjacent to the River Kiso. The tenshu, the tallest tower within the castle, also called the keep, is the only structure remaining today. It was constructed primarily of wood and stone in the yamajiro (mountain castle) style, which provided protection through the natural defences of the terrain.

HAKUSASONSO GARDEN, Kyoto, Japan, 1913–45 CE.

This garden was built by Hashimoto Kansetsu, a famous Nihonga – Japanese-style – artist, and houses his former home and studio. Throughout the garden are small bridges, mossy landscapes and thatched pavilions such as the one shown.

GASSHO-STYLE THATCHED HOUSE, Shirakawa-go, Japan, seventeenth century CE.

Located in the high-mountain historic village of Shirakawa-go, the steep slopes of the thatched roofs of these traditional houses resemble hands pressed together in prayer, hence Gassho-style. Typically three to four storeys, the rooms under the steep pitch of the roof were used to perform work duties. No nails or metal pieces were used to construct the houses; materials such as straw and wood were sourced from the surrounding forests.

SHOSOIN, Todai-ji Temple, Nara, Japan,
eighth century CE.

This is the storehouse for approximately 9,000
treasures of Japanese history. It was constructed
in the simple wooden Azekurazukuri style, with
overlapping triangular beams coming together
at the corners, and true to Japanese tradition,
no nails were used. The entire structure is raised
2.4 m (8 ft) off the ground to protect the holdings
and improve airflow in and around the artefacts.

KIYOMIZU-DERA TEMPLE, Kyoto, Japan, 778 CE.

Translating literally to Pure Water Temple, this
Buddhist temple is sited on top of the Otowa
waterfall and was originally associated with
the Hosso sect, one of the oldest of Japanese
Buddhism. The main hall was built on an
enormous lattice-framed stage, perched 13 m
(43 ft) above the ground, and constructed without
the use of nails in the traditional Japanese style.

EARLY AND CLASSICAL INDIA

CIRCA 300 BCE TO EIGHTEENTH CENTURY CE

Early and Classical Indian architecture is bound up in the religious traditions of the area; in particular, Buddhism, Jainism and Hinduism have all had a profound influence on the development of architectural typologies. Buddhism supported the stupa, typically a burial mound or relic shrine; the stambha, a monumental column; the chaitya hall, a temple for worship usually carved into caves; and the vihara, a monastery. With the decline of Buddhism, Hinduism gave rise to the expansion of the rock-cut temple in an elaborate freestanding form, based on the region in which they were built. Jain architecture also focused on temples and monasteries, similar to the rock-cut temples of Hinduism, but it developed the form into larger temple complexes.

EARLY AND CLASSICAL INDIA KEY FEATURES:

- elaborate and extensive carving
- symbolism
- stupas
- rock-cut temples
- expressive carvings of animals and humans
- pronounced horizontal stone mouldings

SANCHI STUPA, Sanchi Town, Madhya Pradesh, India, 300–100 BCE.

One of the oldest Buddhist monuments in India, the Sanchi Stupa is formed by a hemispherical dome called an anda, perched on a base and surrounded by a square railing, or harmika. There is a relic chamber deep within. The round terrace provides a path for pilgrims to circumambulate the stupa. In front, the ceremonial gate, or toranos, is capped with animal capitals and topped with three architraves with low-relief sculpture depicting the Buddha's life.

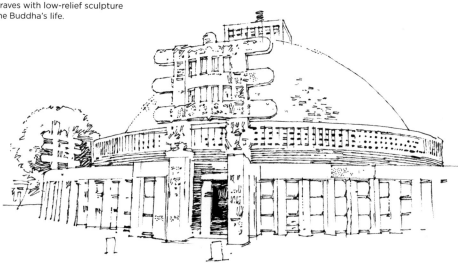

THE GREAT CHAITYA, Karla Caves, Maharashtra, India, 120 CE.

The chaitya, or inner prayer hall, of this Buddhist temple is carved within the Karla Caves and is a fantastic example of Indian rock-cut architecture. The stupa is located at one end of the hall, surrounded by columns carved as animals and humans and topped by a large arched structure of wood.

CHENNAKESAVA TEMPLE, Somanathapura, Karnataka, India, 1258 CE.

This rock-cut Hindu temple is an ornate example of the three-shrine temple of Hoysala architecture, built in the time of the Hoysala Empire. The connected shrines are elevated onto a raised platform that provides a circumambulatory path around the structure. The star-shaped shrines are heavily adorned with elaborate and intricate carvings of Hindu theological representations.

ELLORA CAVES, Maharashtra, India, 600–1000 CE.

The vast Ellora Cave complex has over one hundred basalt rock-cut caves, with monasteries or temples from the Jain, Buddhist, and Hindu religions.

STONE CHARIOT, Vitthala Temple, Hampi, Karnataka, India, sixteenth century CE.

This stone-carved chariot is actually a shrine dedicated to Garuda and is located inside the temple complex. It is not a solid construction but is made of slabs of granite, with the seams of the slabs hidden within the elaborate carving.

SHORE TEMPLE, Mamallapuram, Tamil Nadu, India, 700–728 CE.

Constructed of stacked blocks of granite, this Hindu temple complex is one of the oldest structural stone temples in South India. This five-tiered building sits on a square platform with a small temple in front that constitutes the porch. It is pyramidal in form, with stepped layers reaching up to a cupola and finial, an amalaka, indicating that it is a completed religious structure.

BRAHMESWARA TEMPLE, Bhubaneswar, Orissa, India, 1058 CE.

This Hindu temple dedicated to Shiva is a richly carved sandstone structure with religious iconography on both the interior and exterior. It is a panchatanaya temple, meaning there is a primary shrine, and four sub-shrines located in the four corners of the complex.

NATARAJA TEMPLE, Chidambaram, Tamil Nadu, India, tenth century CE.

This Hindu temple is dedicated to Nataraja – Shiva as a divine dancer – and as a complex is held within four courtyards called prakarams. Connecting the courtyards are nine gateways, gopuram, four of which face each of the cardinal directions and are quite large at seven storeys, with intricate and colourful sculptures.

GOL GUMBAZ, Vijayapura, Karnataka, India, 1626–56 CE, Yaqut of Dubul, architect.

This mausoleum for King Muhammad Adil Shah was built with grey basalt and is in the plan of a square with a seven-storey octagonal tower located at each corner. A large semicircular dome, supported by pendentives on the interior, encases the main open space. At the upper levels of the corner towers are entrances to the gallery located at the base of the dome.

TOMB OF I'TIMAD-UD-DAULAH, Agra, India, 1622–28 CE.

With delicately carved lattice screens called jalis, this beautiful tomb is made completely of marble and has extensive and elaborate examples of pietra dura, ornately cut, polished and colourful stones used to create inlay patterns. The mausoleum sits on a raised plinth of red sandstone and has four octagonal towers, one at each corner, establishing a symmetry and central axis that organizes the building's approach.

MECCA MASJID, Hyderabad, India, 1694 CE.

For one of the largest mosques in India, the grand facade is simple in its form. A long, arched walkway leading to the mosque provides an area for the ritual washing before entering the prayer hall. The minarets located at the corners of the arched facade have circular balconies, each topped with a dome and finial.

TAJ MAHAL, Agra, India, 1632–54 CE, Ustad Ahmad Lahauri, architect.

An enormous mausoleum of white marble, the Taj Mahal stands as a majestic bilaterally symmetrical form of arches and domes, niches and layers, intricate jali lattice carvings and precious stone inlay. The structure is raised on an elevated platform with four minarets, one at each corner, marking the boundaries of the plinth. A large iwan, an arched, semi-domed entrance, marks the entry, while a marble onion dome sits upon a cylindrical drum, adding monumental height to the structure.

2

MEDIEVAL AND RENAISSANCE

EARLY CHRISTIAN AND BYZANTINE

FOURTH CENTURY TO 1453

When Constantine legalized Christianity in 313 CE with the Edict of Milan, there was a need for physical places in which to worship. The most logical approach was to adapt an existing building type that would fit the liturgical needs of Christianity. In the western half of the empire, the Romans adapted the basilica – a long, narrow, colonnaded form with a semicircular protrusion at one end – typically used as a structure in which to conduct business. Since there were no pagan associations with the basilica form, it transitioned easily and the colonnaded, rectilinear space became the nave and side aisles, while the semicircular area developed into the altar.

In 324 CE, with Constantine's defeat of Licinius, the ruler of the eastern portion of the empire, the capital was moved to the Greek town of Byzantium and labelled the 'new Rome'. Renamed Constantinople, this area developed its own special Byzantine architectural style that reflected changes in liturgical practices. It focused less on the order of a long nave and side aisles and more on a centralized practice of worship, reflecting the importance put upon the procession of the clergy. Thus, many structures developed with the organizing principle of a centralized dome.

EARLY CHRISTIAN KEY FEATURES:

- basilica form
- interior colonnade with apse at end
- rectangular in plan
- three or five aisles
- central nave typically taller than the side aisles

BYZANTINE KEY FEATURES:

- centralized plan
- pendentive dome
- rich, mosaic interiors of religious symbolism

BASILICA OF SANTA SABINA, Rome, Italy, 422–32.

This Early Christian church, located on the Aventine Hill in Rome, is the oldest Roman basilica to survive and maintains its original traits, such as the rectangular plan lined with columns. The exterior of the church looks much as it did in the fifth century, with windows made of selenite and a clear definition of the organization of the church, with the rectilinear portion capped at one end with a semicircular apse.

BASILICA OF SAINT-PIERRE-AUX-NONNAINS, Metz, France, fourth century.

This basilica is one of the most outstanding remaining examples of late Roman architecture in the world. The structure was originally built as a gymnasium, part of a Roman spa in the fourth century. In the seventh century it was converted to a Benedictine church. It is an excellent example of the conversion of the secular Roman basilica form into a religious structure.

BASILICA OF SANT'APOLLINARE NUOVO, Ravenna, Italy, 505.

Though basilican in form and thus a formal representation of an Early Christian church, this basilica features mosaics in the interior – along the top of the arches facing the nave – in the Byzantine style.

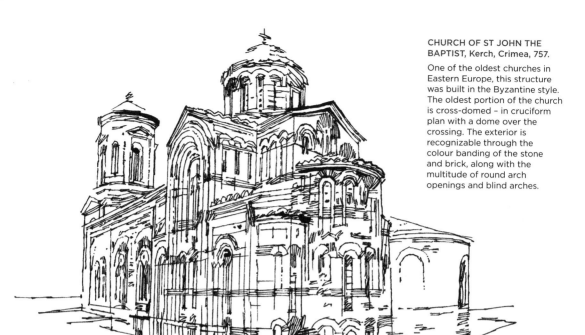

CHURCH OF ST JOHN THE BAPTIST, Kerch, Crimea, 757.

One of the oldest churches in Eastern Europe, this structure was built in the Byzantine style. The oldest portion of the church is cross-domed – in cruciform plan with a dome over the crossing. The exterior is recognizable through the colour banding of the stone and brick, along with the multitude of round arch openings and blind arches.

SANTA COSTANZA, Rome, Italy, fourth century.

Originally thought to be a mausoleum built by Constantine for his daughter, this Early Christian building is very different to a traditional basilican structure. Santa Costanza is round in form with a dome encircled by an ambulatory consisting of twelve pairs of granite Composite columns. Windows surrounding the drum of the dome light the centre of the space, in stark contrast to the darkness of the surrounding ambulatory.

HAGIA EIRENE, Topkapi Palace, Istanbul, Turkey, 532.

This Byzantine church is unique in that it was never converted into a mosque. As such it maintains the ordered, characteristic basilican plan, with the addition of a dome adjacent to the apse end. Thus, we see the traditional Early Christian rectilinear plan on the lower level, with the addition of the Byzantine dome form on top.

CHURCH OF SAINT GEORGE ROTUNDA, Sofia, Bulgaria, fourth century.

This Early Christian round brick rotunda is a cylindrical domed form. The circular central space under the dome is surrounded by four semicircular apses. The building is the oldest still standing in Sofia, and the interior boasts multiple layers of frescoes dating from different centuries.

HAGIA SOPHIA, Istanbul, Turkey, 360–537.

Hagia Sophia - translating to divine wisdom – stands as one of the finest examples of Byzantine architecture. The exterior, in modest brick, expresses the diversity of the interior. Inside, the space is dominated by the massive saucer dome, supported by half-domes on two sides and four large piers. An oval, formed by the shaping of the inner arcade, frames the space of the dome at ground level. Multiple levels of arcades of varying rhythm rise above.

BASILICA OF SAN VITALE, Ravenna, Italy, 547.

Unusual in its octagonal plan, this church is organized around a central dome. An internally expressed octagon is surrounded with arches, creating a series of arcades encompassing the centre space. The brick exterior remains largely as it did in the sixth century and is modest in decoration. This early example of flying buttresses also constructed in brick is worth noting. The church houses the most significant collection of Byzantine mosaics found outside of Istanbul.

HAGIA SOPHIA, Thessaloniki, Greece,
eighth century.

The Hagia Sophia in Thessaloniki – not to be
confused with that in Istanbul – is a clear example
of the use of the Byzantine pendentive dome,
created when a circular dome is placed over
a square-shaped space. Pendentives are the
triangle-shaped portions of a sphere that transfer
the weight of the dome down to the piers that
support it.

ISLAMIC
SEVENTH TO NINETEENTH CENTURIES

Islamic architecture is most readily expressed through buildings associated with the religion of Islam, and predominantly through the mosque, a place of worship, or madrassa, a place of learning. The complexity of the Islamic decorative patterns defines the beauty of many of these structures. These extraordinary geometric designs are made from four basic shapes: circle, square, star and multi-sided polygon. Focusing on the importance of unity and order, Islamic artists combined and blended these forms to create a unique decorative style. Additional elaborate, surface, arabesque decoration was designed with scrolling and intertwining foliage. Ornamental vaulting, known as muqarnas, was widely used and is a form of honeycomb vaulting.

The architecture developed for the practice of Islam referenced some typical characteristics of Christian architecture, such as domes and arcades, with fundamental changes reflecting the needs of the Muslim practice. Large courtyard spaces for group prayer were added, as well as the mihrab – a niche in the wall of the mosque that indicates the direction of prayer towards Mecca. Minarets were important elements as well, aiding the call to prayer and providing a strong visual reminder of the presence of Islam.

ISLAMIC KEY FEATURES:

- **domes**
- **minarets**
- **pointed arches**
- **enclosed courtyards**
- **geometric decoration**
- **arabesque decoration**
- **muqarnas**

SULTAN AHMED MOSQUE (Blue Mosque), Istanbul, Turkey, 1609–16, Sedefkâr Mehmed Aga, architect.

The Blue Mosque – named after the abundance of blue tiles on the interior – along with Hagia Sophia dominates the skyline of Istanbul, with five main domes, eight secondary domes, and six minarets. The structure incorporates some Byzantine elements along with traditional Islamic architecture. The dome of the mosque features pendentives, much like the Hagia Sophia church, while the complex is dominated by two main spaces: the prayer hall under the dome, and the spacious exterior courtyard used for ablutions.

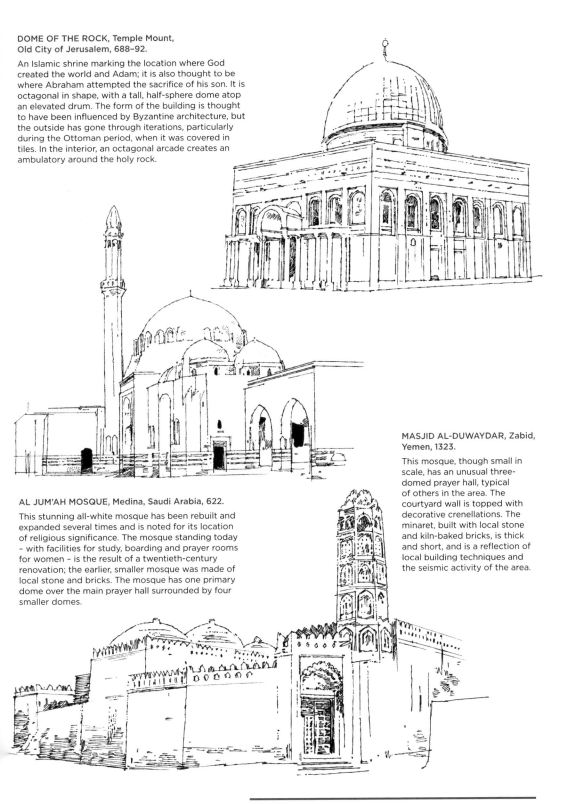

DOME OF THE ROCK, Temple Mount, Old City of Jerusalem, 688–92.

An Islamic shrine marking the location where God created the world and Adam; it is also thought to be where Abraham attempted the sacrifice of his son. It is octagonal in shape, with a tall, half-sphere dome atop an elevated drum. The form of the building is thought to have been influenced by Byzantine architecture, but the outside has gone through iterations, particularly during the Ottoman period, when it was covered in tiles. In the interior, an octagonal arcade creates an ambulatory around the holy rock.

MASJID AL-DUWAYDAR, Zabid, Yemen, 1323.

This mosque, though small in scale, has an unusual three-domed prayer hall, typical of others in the area. The courtyard wall is topped with decorative crenellations. The minaret, built with local stone and kiln-baked bricks, is thick and short, and is a reflection of local building techniques and the seismic activity of the area.

AL JUM'AH MOSQUE, Medina, Saudi Arabia, 622.

This stunning all-white mosque has been rebuilt and expanded several times and is noted for its location of religious significance. The mosque standing today – with facilities for study, boarding and prayer rooms for women – is the result of a twentieth-century renovation; the earlier, smaller mosque was made of local stone and bricks. The mosque has one primary dome over the main prayer hall surrounded by four smaller domes.

ALHAMBRA, Granada, Spain, 1238–1358, Muhammed Al-Ahmar,
architect.

An Islamic palace and fortress built for a Muslim emir in Spain, the
Alhambra – 'the red one', a reference to the colour of the outer walls –
is actually a series of interconnected palaces and courtyards, and is
considered a masterpiece of Moorish architecture.

This courtyard, the Court of the Myrtles, is one of six principal courts at
the Alhambra. The pool and arcade of arched grille lattice frames the
view to the Medieval tower beyond. The pool and courtyard systems
were used as part of the cooling strategy for the palaces.

MOSQUE-MADRASSA OF SULTAN HASSAN,
Cairo, Egypt, 1356–63.

Both a place of worship and a school – mosque
and madrassa, respectively – the compound also
contains a mausoleum and is noted for both its
large scale and the variety of construction and
decoration techniques, largely attributed to the
sheer number of craftsmen required to achieve
a building of this magnitude.

ALHAMBRA, Granada, Spain, 1238–1358,
Muhammed Al-Ahmar, architect.

An oblong courtyard, the Court of the Lions, has
at its centre a fountain supported by lion figures.
This view, from the courtyard pavilion, displays the
incredible colonnade of elaborately carved filigree
arched walls. Note the cubiform column capitals;
they are the geometric result of an intersection of
a cube and a hemisphere, and are square at the
top and round at the bottom.

GREAT MOSQUE OF DAMASCUS, Damascus, Syria, 708-15.

The form of the prayer hall is similar to that of an Early Christian basilica, except that there is no apse to face during worship. Instead, worshippers face the mihrab, a semicircular niche indicating the direction of prayer – the qibla. The hall of worship is divided into three aisles by rows of arcades with Corinthian capitals. The elevation of the transept is visible from the courtyard and marks the entrance to the prayer hall.

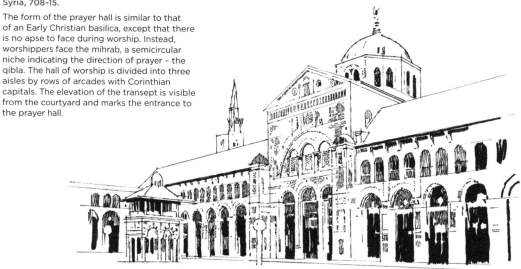

SHAH MOSQUE, Isfahan, Iran, 1611–29.

The iwan – three-sided entrance portal – of this Iranian mosque is a beautiful example of the use of muqarnas, a decorative device in stalactite form (not structural), that is used to visually transition between domed spaces and straight walls. This mosque in Isfahan has four iwans facing a central public courtyard.

MOSQUE OF AMR IBN AL-AS, Cairo, Egypt, 641–42.

As the first mosque built in Egypt, the Mosque of Amr ibn al-As went through multiple phases of rebuilding up to the twentieth century. The arcades along the southern wall are the oldest remaining and date to the ninth century. This view of the courtyard shows the central feature of the ablution fountain, where the ritual washing is performed prior to prayer.

MASJID AL-QIBLATAYN (Mosque of the Two Qiblas), Medina, Saudi Arabia, 623.

With twin domes and twin minarets, the main prayer hall of this mosque adheres to a strict symmetrical geometry. The name, Mosque of the Two Qiblas refers to the change of direction of prayer from Jerusalem to Mecca. The main dome is lifted on a drum of windows providing light directly above the mihrab in the prayer hall below.

ROMANESQUE
ELEVENTH TO EARLY THIRTEENTH CENTURIES

A direct extension of the building techniques developed in Rome, the Romanesque style of architecture advanced across Europe virtually simultaneously, with each region developing slightly different characteristics while the overarching components remained the same. The principles of Romanesque architecture were used to design a wide variety of building types, but it is the church that remains the predominant example. Churches strived to be larger to accommodate the expansion of monastic life during Medieval times. In order to achieve that goal, the walls, piers, and columns had to be thicker as they were bearing the load of the structure, and this feature alone is the easiest way to identify a Romanesque building. Other essential elements, such as round or semicircular arches, paired openings of two arched windows and articulated apses, are universal attributes of Romanesque architecture.

ROMANESQUE KEY FEATURES:

- thick walls
- thick, heavy piers and columns
- symmetrical plans
- round, semicircular arches
- barrel vaults and simple groin vaults
- predominant towers
- arcades, both open and blind
- articulated apses

CHURCH OF SAN MILLAN, Segovia, Spain, 1111–24.

With its visible articulated apses – one primary and three secondary – this Romanesque church is simple in its organization. Its entrance is from the side, after passing through a beautiful, staid, round arch arcade porch. The plenitudinous tower pre-dates the church and is Mozarabic – a building style of Christians on the Iberian Peninsula.

BAMBERG CATHEDRAL, Bamberg, Germany, thirteenth century.

Due to the extensive nature of alterations over time, the cathedral exhibits multiple architectural styles, primarily Romanesque and Gothic. This main entrance portal, the Fürstenportal, is only open on holy days. Romanesque doorways typically consist of an arched opening with multiple receding planes and a continuous abacus – a horizonal plane at the top of a column capital. When there are twelve receding planes, as in the example here, they represent the twelve apostles of Christ. The sculptural work began during the Romanesque period and was completed during the Gothic.

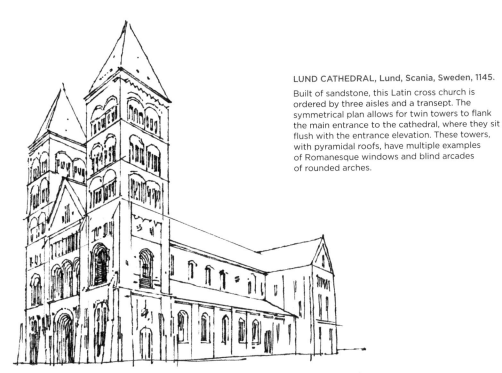

LUND CATHEDRAL, Lund, Scania, Sweden, 1145.

Built of sandstone, this Latin cross church is ordered by three aisles and a transept. The symmetrical plan allows for twin towers to flank the main entrance to the cathedral, where they sit flush with the entrance elevation. These towers, with pyramidal roofs, have multiple examples of Romanesque windows and blind arcades of rounded arches.

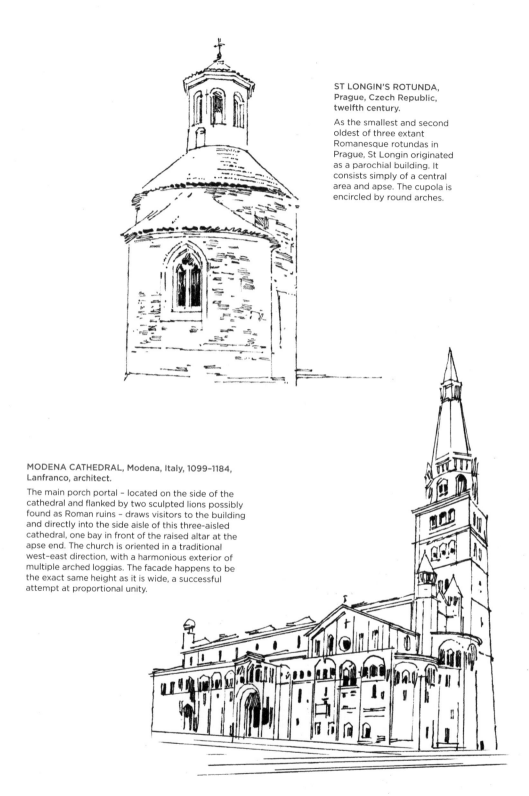

**ST LONGIN'S ROTUNDA,
Prague, Czech Republic,
twelfth century.**

As the smallest and second
oldest of three extant
Romanesque rotundas in
Prague, St Longin originated
as a parochial building. It
consists simply of a central
area and apse. The cupola is
encircled by round arches.

**MODENA CATHEDRAL, Modena, Italy, 1099–1184,
Lanfranco, architect.**

The main porch portal – located on the side of the
cathedral and flanked by two sculpted lions possibly
found as Roman ruins – draws visitors to the building
and directly into the side aisle of this three-aisled
cathedral, one bay in front of the raised altar at the
apse end. The church is oriented in a traditional
west–east direction, with a harmonious exterior of
multiple arched loggias. The facade happens to be
the exact same height as it is wide, a successful
attempt at proportional unity.

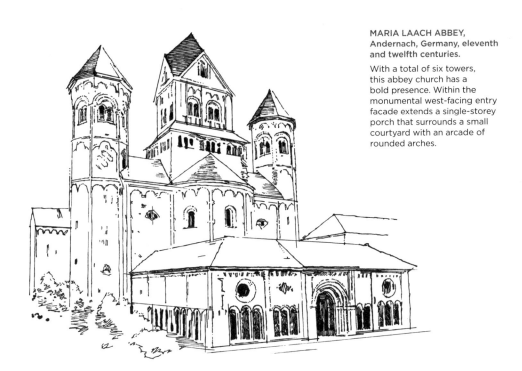

MARIA LAACH ABBEY, Andernach, Germany, eleventh and twelfth centuries.

With a total of six towers, this abbey church has a bold presence. Within the monumental west-facing entry facade extends a single-storey porch that surrounds a small courtyard with an arcade of rounded arches.

LESSAY ABBEY, Lessay, Manche, France, eleventh century.

Displaying a Latin cross form, this abbey church follows the typical layout of a Romanesque church, with two aisles, one on each side of the nave, a transept and apse. A square tower rises up at the crossing of nave and transept. What is most remarkable about this church is the use of a rib vault system that would later become prevalent in Gothic architecture. On the exterior, pier buttresses were used to help carry the weight of the roof, adding to the visual effect and actual mass of this structure.

FOUNTAINS ABBEY, Aldfield, England, 1132.

Twelfth-century stepped Romanesque arches from this large abbey founded along the River Skell are likely to be the remains of a portal entrance to a cloister at the abbey.

ABBEY OF SAINT-ÉTIENNE, Caen, France, 1067.

The sombre facade, absent of any decoration, appears extraordinarily tall, with two towers seemingly taller than the main volume of the church. Romanesque arched openings are the only features aside from four pier buttresses. The twin towers are terminated by thirteenth-century spires.

BASILICA OF SAINT-SERNIN, Toulouse, France, 1080–1120.

The bell tower rising up from the intersection of the nave and the transept is separated into five tiers. The lower three tiers are Romanesque, as evidenced by the rounded arches. The upper two levels are from the thirteenth century, with the spire added during the fifteenth century. The chevet – a choir made of radiating chapels – clearly visible here, is formed from nine chapels, five adjacent to the apse and four located in the transept.

ABBEY CHURCH OF ST JAMES,
Lébény, Hungary, 1208–12.

With characteristics such as the paired arched openings within a larger arch, small ocular window, strong west-facing edifice and stepped arched portal, this Hungarian church is a clear example of Romanesque architecture. Its square towers are each topped with a Rhenish helm roof, also typical of the style in this region. This type of roof is a pyramid in plan, but as there are gables on each of the four sides of the tower, each plane of the pyramid is actually a geometric rhomboid.

GURK CATHEDRAL, Gurk, Austria, twelfth century.

One of the most significant examples of Romanesque architecture in Austria, Gurk Cathedral stands with austere dignity. The twin towers of the westwork – monumental west-facing entrance facade – are topped with onion domes added in the seventeenth century. Visible here are the three apse forms directly adjacent to the crossing of the broad transept.

ABBEY CHURCH OF SAINT-SAVIN-SUR-GARTEMPE, Poitou, France, mid-eleventh century.

With its well-balanced spatial volumes, this abbey church is in a crucifix form with a square tower at the crossing between nave and transept. The church has been dubbed 'The Romanesque Sistine Chapel' due to the quality and quantity of eleventh- and twelfth-century frescoes found in the interior. From the exterior, the choir, its ambulatory and five radial chapels – the chevet – are visible, as well as the polygonal apse.

GOTHIC
MID-TWELFTH TO SIXTEENTH CENTURIES

Originating in France with the design and construction of the Basilica of St Denis – considered to be the first use of structural and stylistic traits of Gothic architecture – the style evolved from Romanesque and strived for taller and taller religious structures that evoked a feeling of reaching for the heavens. In order to accomplish this goal, architects devised structural systems that no longer relied on the thickness of walls, columns and piers to displace the weight of the building. Innovations such as rib vaults and flying buttresses essentially redirected the load and dispersed it to different structural elements. This allowed for a significantly lighter construction method and provided opportunity for increased glass, light and delicate and intricate ornamentation. This expression of lightness ultimately became synonymous with the ornate aesthetic associated with Gothic architecture.

GOTHIC KEY FEATURES:
- pointed arches
- flying buttresses
- rib vaults
- thinner, lighter structures
- taller nave spaces
- abundant stained-glass windows
- plate tracery and bar tracery
- more efficient load-bearing capabilities
- intense decoration
- pinnacles and thin spires

AMIENS CATHEDRAL, Amiens, France, 1220–70, Robert of Luzarches, Thomas and Regnault de Cormont, architects.

The three entrance portals dominate the organization of the cathedral facade, replicating the interior. Rising above the pointed arches of the portals is a gallery of sculpted kings residing in niches in a horizontal band across the entire facade. The rose window finishes the centre section with an open arcade and a series of pinnacles above. The towers here are not twin towers, as the last tier of each one was finished during a different period and does not reflect a symmetrical approach.

COLOGNE CATHEDRAL, Cologne, Germany, 1248–1473.

Typical of many Gothic cathedrals, the plan is a Latin cross with two side aisles and a central nave. The cathedral is one of the highest Gothic vaults in the world, and the structural distribution of this weight is through flying buttresses. With its twin towers, the facade is a composition of highly ornate tracery, pinnacles, openwork stone spires, finials and pointed arches. Work was halted on the cathedral in 1473 and the building was left unfinished until the nineteenth century.

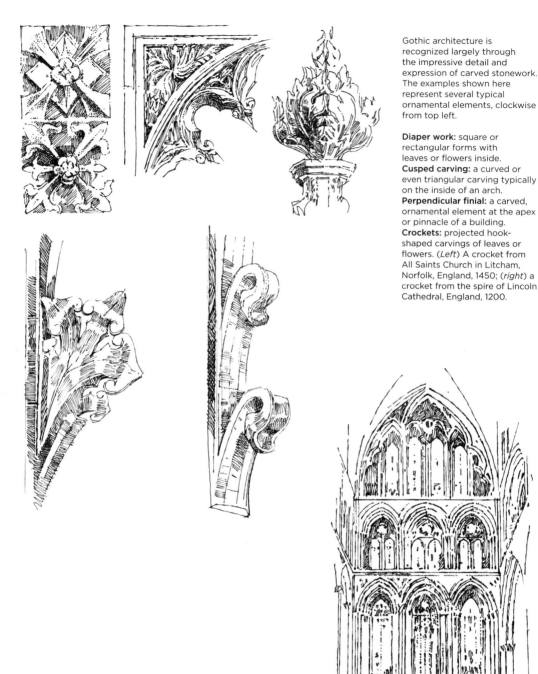

Gothic architecture is recognized largely through the impressive detail and expression of carved stonework. The examples shown here represent several typical ornamental elements, clockwise from top left.

Diaper work: square or rectangular forms with leaves or flowers inside.
Cusped carving: a curved or even triangular carving typically on the inside of an arch.
Perpendicular finial: a carved, ornamental element at the apex or pinnacle of a building.
Crockets: projected hook-shaped carvings of leaves or flowers. (*Left*) A crocket from All Saints Church in Litcham, Norfolk, England, 1450; (*right*) a crocket from the spire of Lincoln Cathedral, England, 1200.

SALISBURY CATHEDRAL, Salisbury, England, 1220–58.

The north transept is tall and narrow; a geometric reflection of the volume of the nave. Three tiers divide the height of the space, with elongated lancet windows at the first and third levels. Purbeck marble – found south of Dorset, England– forms the engaged colonette clusters supporting the arched openings framing elaborate stained-glass windows.

DOM TOWER OF UTRECHT, Utrecht, the Netherlands, 1321–82, John of Hainaut, architect.

Originally attached to a cathedral, the tower now stands alone as one of the highest church towers in the Netherlands. It has three primary segments: the first two sections are rectangular with open, pointed archwork and some tracery decoration. The top section is an open, light and elegant lantern featuring delicate arched pinnacles at the skyline.

LINCOLN CATHEDRAL, Lincoln, England, 1185–1311.

The rib vaulting system within the cathedral is unusual, sporting multiple types of traditional and experimental vaults. There are continuous and discontinuous ridge rib vaults, quadripartite vaults, sexpartite vaults and other asymmetrical vault systems. Those shown here from the Angel Choir radiate upwards from clustered columns that form the arched side aisles.

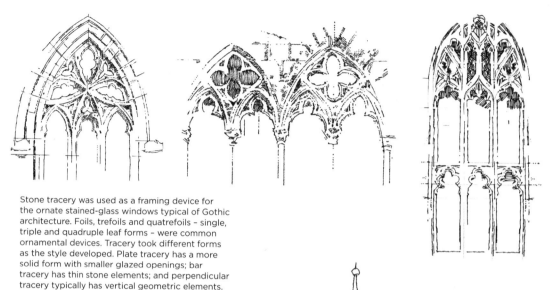

Stone tracery was used as a framing device for the ornate stained-glass windows typical of Gothic architecture. Foils, trefoils and quatrefoils – single, triple and quadruple leaf forms – were common ornamental devices. Tracery took different forms as the style developed. Plate tracery has a more solid form with smaller glazed openings; bar tracery has thin stone elements; and perpendicular tracery typically has vertical geometric elements.

MINISTER OF THE HOLY CROSS, Schwäbisch Gmünd, Germany, 1315–1521, Heinrich Parler the Elder, architect.

The round choir at the north apse end of the church is a magnificent example of Late Gothic architectural stonework. Designed by one of the prominent families of Gothic architecture in Germany, the bar tracery, quatrefoil balustrades and pinnacles define the elaborate nature of this choir.

**ORVIETO CATHEDRAL,
Orvieto, Umbria, Italy,
1290–1591, Arnolfo di Cambio
and Lorenzo Maitani, architects.**

The beautifully symmetrical
facade of Orvieto Cathedral is
attributed to Maitani. However,
others contributed elements;
Orcagna, an architect and
sculptor, created the elaborate
rose window. The facade is
organized in three bays, with
rich mosaics of gold at each
level. Sculptural niches surround
the rose window, rising up
to mosaic-clad gables with
pinnacles reaching to the sky.

**TOWN HALL, Schotten, Hesse,
Germany, fifteenth century.**

This Late Gothic town hall
was constructed in half-timber
work. This particular method
of building consists of timber
frames filled with intermediary
material such as brick, wattle
and daub or plaster. Typically,
squared oak timbers are used,
with a slightly projecting
second level to help balance
the load requirements of the
upper levels. Exposed angle
bracing, as seen here, is
characteristic of German
half-timbered structures.

KING'S COLLEGE CHAPEL,
Cambridge, England, 1446–1515.

The extraordinary fan vaulting
of the chapel demonstrates the
geometric gymnastics required
from this structural system. Ribs
rise up from central points and
radiate (fan) out with equal
curvatures and at equal
distances, forming a semi-cone
shape at the vault surface.

**CHURCH OF ST MARY THE
VIRGIN,** Tilty, Essex, England,
thirteenth century.

Known for the delicate tracery
of the east window, this parish
church is primarily from the
thirteenth century, but was built
over several different time
periods, evidenced by the
stepped volumes. The larger
of the volumes, made of local
stone, sports pilaster buttresses
to support the structure.

NORTH ROSE WINDOW, Notre-Dame de Paris, Paris, France, 1163–1345.

Rose windows became increasingly popular as tracery artisans became more and more skilled at the delicate stonework. Typically formed in a radiating pattern, the intricate tracery supports the lead-framed stained glass.

THE CHURCH OF OUR LADY OF BLOXHAM, Bloxham, England, twelfth to fourteenth centuries.

One of four crocketed pinnacles surrounding the tapering square tower of this spire.

MILAN CATHEDRAL, Milan, Italy, 1387–1965, Simone da Orsenigo, architect.

With five naves – one central and four side – this cathedral's interior form directly influences the organization of the facade. The highly articulated, layered facade has 3,400 statues, 700 figures and 135 gargoyles. An unusual feature is the sheer number of delicate open pinnacles that grace the roof line. Upon close inspection, it should be noted that on the tops of the crocketed pinnacles are statuary of saints. Over seventy-seven architects worked on the cathedral over multiple centuries.

MEDIEVAL FORTIFICATIONS
LATE ELEVENTH TO SIXTEENTH CENTURIES

Built with defence functionality in mind, Medieval fortifications were originally developed to protect the nobility from marauding forces. Early examples included a keep – a fortified tower on an earthen mound – and a bailey – an open space surrounded by fortified walls. The keep was the last position of protection and therefore considered the most secure. As different forms of weaponry developed, so too did the nature and utilitarian function of fortification architecture. Focus shifted away from primary protection of the keep, and Medieval fortifications began to evolve through the improvement of the fortified wall. Concentric castles developed with features such as concentric fortified walls – at least one outer lower wall with a higher inner wall – round towers to provide better views, multiple gatehouses and the addition of a moat and drawbridge. Medieval fortifications also included walls that encompassed entire cities. Examples of these types of fortification can be found all over the world, including China, England, Canada and Croatia.

MEDIEVAL FORTIFICATIONS KEY FEATURES:

- thick, defensive walls
- small, narrow openings
- battlements, also known as crenellated parapets
- bastions
- towers
- gatehouses
- moats
- keeps
- arrow loops

ALCÁZAR OF SEGOVIA, Segovia, Spain, thirteenth and fourteenth centuries.

Built at the confluence of two rivers, the castle sits high above the city on a rocky outcrop. Originally built as a Roman fort – only the foundations remain – the form is said to resemble the prow of a mighty ship. The distinctive thin, pointed spires were added at a later date to reflect trends in other European castles.

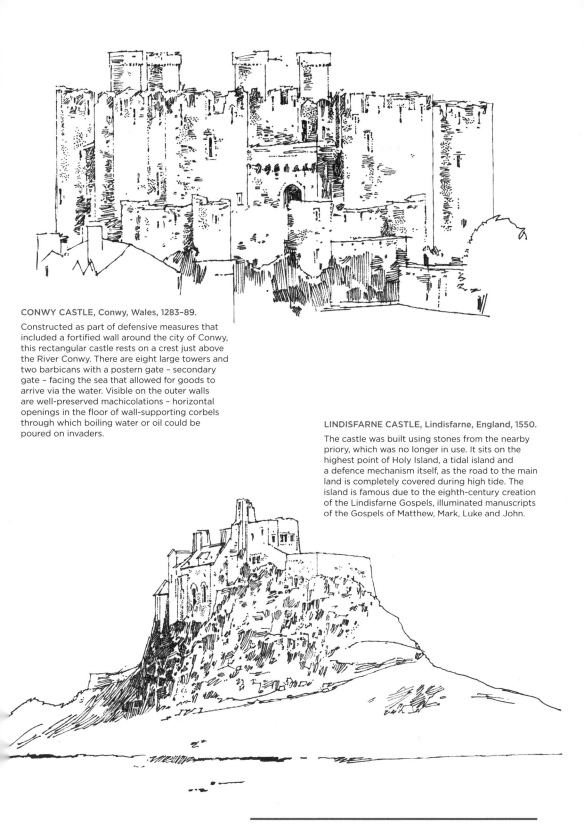

CONWY CASTLE, Conwy, Wales, 1283–89.

Constructed as part of defensive measures that included a fortified wall around the city of Conwy, this rectangular castle rests on a crest just above the River Conwy. There are eight large towers and two barbicans with a postern gate – secondary gate – facing the sea that allowed for goods to arrive via the water. Visible on the outer walls are well-preserved machicolations – horizontal openings in the floor of wall-supporting corbels through which boiling water or oil could be poured on invaders.

LINDISFARNE CASTLE, Lindisfarne, England, 1550.

The castle was built using stones from the nearby priory, which was no longer in use. It sits on the highest point of Holy Island, a tidal island and a defence mechanism itself, as the road to the main land is completely covered during high tide. The island is famous due to the eighth-century creation of the Lindisfarne Gospels, illuminated manuscripts of the Gospels of Matthew, Mark, Luke and John.

CASTILLO DE LA MOTA,
Medina del Campo, Spain,
fourteenth and fifteenth
centuries.

Located on a hill – mota – this
particular castle is noted for
its large outer barbicans. The
barbican is a fortified gateway,
or technically any tower
positioned over a gate or part
of the fortified wall, and was
used for defensive purposes.
Here, the barbicans are round,
a defence measure as corners
were more difficult to defend.

CARCASSONNE FORTIFIED CITY,
Carcassonne, France.

With over 3.2 km (2 miles) of a double-walled
fortification complete with fifty-two defensive
towers, this Medieval fortified city has been
occupied since the third century. From the
eleventh century onwards, multiple significant
additions have been made, including a
controversial full restoration by Eugène
Viollet-le-Duc during the nineteenth century.

Right: Even the gates had defensive elements,
providing holes for archers.

FRAMLINGHAM CASTLE, Framlingham, England, twelfth and thirteenth centuries.

As early as the twelfth century, a motte and bailey castle was located on this site. A motte is a raised area of ground upon which a keep is typically placed, and a bailey is an accompanying enclosed courtyard that is defendable. During the late twelfth and early thirteenth centuries, the castle that stands today was built. Unique in that there is no central keep, the castle boasts an encircling defensive wall with mural towers – square defensive towers built within the wall.

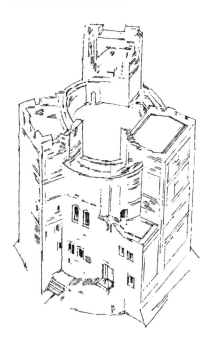

ORFORD CASTLE KEEP, Orford, England, 1165–73.

An unusual design, the Orford Castle keep is round in form with three rectangular towers intersecting the circular structure. The proportional system of the construction of the tower is thought to be based on the one-to-the-root-of-two ratio commonly used in English church design of the same period.

HEDINGHAM CASTLE KEEP, Castle Hedingham, England, 1140.

This keep is almost a perfect square in plan, a common form for a Norman keep, and has five floors, including a double-height Great Hall and a circular stair in one of the corner towers.

BODIAM CASTLE, Robertsbridge, England, 1385.

This moated castle has no central keep; instead there are numerous chambers built around the defensive walls and inner courts. Considered a quadrangular, or courtyard, castle, it is largely rectangular in form with a central courtyard.

CARDIFF CASTLE, Cardiff, Wales, late eleventh century.

Built atop Roman walls, the castle was constructed by Normans as a defensive structure and part of their quest west into Wales. With multiple revisions and additions over hundreds of years, the primary changes occurred during the eighteenth century, when it was largely remodelled in the Gothic Revival style. The walls of the castle are occupiable and, during World War II, were used as air raid shelters, holding up to 1,800 people at one time.

WALLS OF ÁVILA, Ávila, Spain, eleventh to fourteenth centuries.

The Medieval walls of Ávila are punctuated with eighty-eight semicircular towers at regular intervals. The rough stone walls are approximately 3 m (10 ft) thick and 12 m (40 ft) tall with nine separate gates. Typical Medieval defensive crenellation is visible along the top. The walls vary in height in response to their relative proximity to natural features of defence: for instance, the south side wall is lower because of the slope of the land upon which it was built.

PREDJAMA CASTLE, Predjama, Slovenia, 1570.

Built into a 122-m-high (400 ft) vertical cliff underneath the original Medieval fortification, Predjama Castle is considered the world's largest cave castle. Secret tunnels from the castle, through the cave, and out into the countryside ensured the survival of families during times of siege.

RENAISSANCE
FIFTEENTH TO SEVENTEENTH CENTURIES

With the advent of the Renaissance – literally defined as 'rebirth' – came the cultural movement of returning to the models of literature, art and architecture from antiquity. For architects, this idea was first promoted in Leon Battista Alberti's *On the Art of Building in Ten Books*, which became the reference tome of the Renaissance movement in architecture. It described architecture not just as a utilitarian objective, but as an art with a significant humanistic element. Predominant in Italy, the style was propagated throughout Europe and England, and focused on proportion, symmetry and the repetition of regular parts as established by the architecture of Ancient Rome and Greece. While the Renaissance saw a shift to a conscious revival of ancient forms, these were then blended with current principles of architectural ideals.

CA' D'ORO, Venice, Italy, 1428–30, Giovanni and Bartolomeo Bon, architects.

With an offset symmetrical facade, this Venetian palace is divided into three levels: the lower loggia, characterized by a large, round central arch with pointed arches surrounding; the middle balcony with balustrade and quatrefoil details; and the upper balcony with a scaled reduction of similar features from the middle balcony. The palace incorporates Gothic, Islamic and Byzantine elements, making it a unique transitional piece of early Venetian Renaissance architecture.

PALAZZO MEDICI, Florence, Italy, 1444–84, Michelozzo di Bartolomeo, architect.

The elevation of the palace is in three classic parts: a rusticated base with two additional levels, with a much finer treatment of the stone as the facade moves upwards. The top of the building has a magnificent cornice with a broad corbelled overhang that balances visually with the weight of the base. The use of gradating stone accentuates the visual relationship between the levels of the building and makes it appear grander by the illusion of stretching the facade.

SCUOLA GRANDE DI SAN MARCO, Venice, Italy, 1260, Pietro Lombardo, Mauro Codussi and Bartolomeo Bon, architects.

This grand facade with highly ornamental niches at the skyline is a Renaissance marvel of marble construction. Of particular note is the marble work at the ground floor. All of the three-dimensional archways and portals you see, save the two darkened doors, are actually trompe-l'oeil and are not receding into space. Trompe-l'oeil was a technique used to create an optical illusion of three dimensions on a two-dimensional surface. Perspective drawings were popular during the Renaissance as more and more artists strived for a representation of realism.

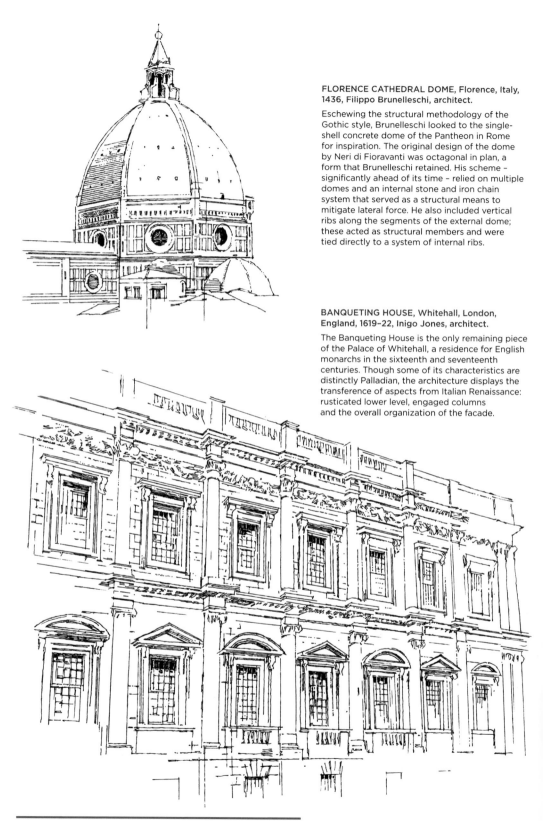

FLORENCE CATHEDRAL DOME, Florence, Italy, 1436, Filippo Brunelleschi, architect.

Eschewing the structural methodology of the Gothic style, Brunelleschi looked to the single-shell concrete dome of the Pantheon in Rome for inspiration. The original design of the dome by Neri di Fioravanti was octagonal in plan, a form that Brunelleschi retained. His scheme – significantly ahead of its time – relied on multiple domes and an internal stone and iron chain system that served as a structural means to mitigate lateral force. He also included vertical ribs along the segments of the external dome; these acted as structural members and were tied directly to a system of internal ribs.

BANQUETING HOUSE, Whitehall, London, England, 1619–22, Inigo Jones, architect.

The Banqueting House is the only remaining piece of the Palace of Whitehall, a residence for English monarchs in the sixteenth and seventeenth centuries. Though some of its characteristics are distinctly Palladian, the architecture displays the transference of aspects from Italian Renaissance: rusticated lower level, engaged columns and the overall organization of the facade.

CHÂTEAU DE BLOIS, Blois, Loir-et-Cher, France, thirteenth to seventeenth centuries.

This polygonal ceremonial staircase appears simultaneously light and heavy. With finely balustraded edges that shift in design from the lower to upper levels, fashionable Renaissance attributes of figures, shells, medallions and references to antiquity abound. The staircase moves in and out of the facade and allows for a multitude of views in and out as users move vertically along the path.

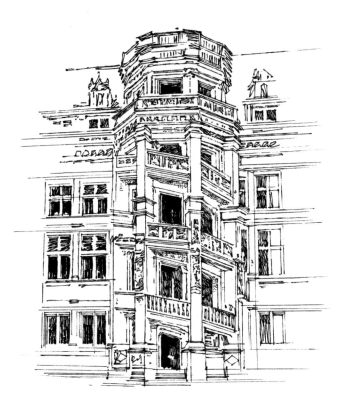

TORRE DEI LAMBERTI, Verona, Italy, 1172

Originally constructed in 1172, this 84-m (275-ft) bell tower was struck by lightning and collapsed in 1403. Reconstruction began in 1448 and was completed in 1463. A clock was added in 1798. The tower is in two forms: the lower portion is square in plan, while the upper portion is octagonal and of a similar style to towers in Venice. The break in brick style is evident and indicates a change in material from tuff blocks and brick to brick only.

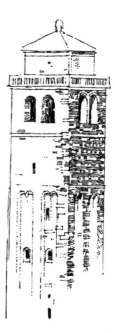

With brick as the material, their square profiles and pyramid-shaped roofs, these campaniles – bell towers – of Venice display classical characteristics of Renaissance architecture.

BASILICA OF SANT'ANDREA, Mantua, Italy, 1472–1790, Leon Battista Alberti, architect.

With its large vaulted structure on the facade, Alberti corresponded the exterior of the building to the interior. The central nave is crowned by a large barrel vault, which, along with the similar facade element, references the triumphal arch.

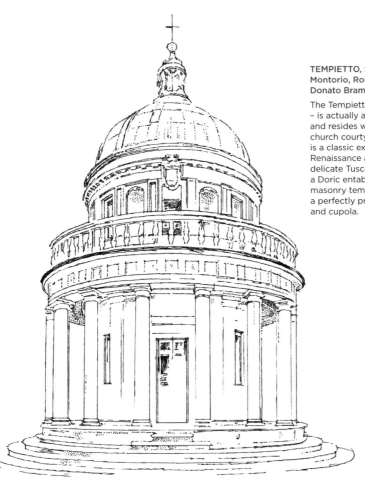

TEMPIETTO, San Pietro in Montorio, Rome, Italy, 1502, Donato Bramante, architect.

The Tempietto – small temple – is actually a memorial tomb and resides within a slender church courtyard. This structure is a classic example of High Renaissance architecture, with delicate Tuscan columns and a Doric entablature. The round masonry temple is topped with a perfectly proportioned dome and cupola.

CHÂTEAU DE CHAMBORD, Chambord, Loir-et-Cher, France, 1519–47, Domenico da Cortona, architect.

An example of French Renaissance architecture, the layout of this château is a mix of both French and Italian styles of collecting rooms together into suites. It is arranged as a castle with a large outer wall and central courtyard, though was not designed with any defensive intentions. The animated roof line of the château boasts multiple types of towers and chimneys, which combine as a contrast to the mass of the building below.

MANNERISM
EARLY SIXTEENTH TO EARLY SEVENTEENTH CENTURIES

Mannerism came about as a reaction to the strict reference to antiquity of the Renaissance and provided architects with some artistic freedom in the development of their new works. These architectural experiments challenged assumptions of Classicism by adjusting and distorting architectural proportions, rhythm and order. Mannerist architects deliberately sought to challenge expectations by creating works that confused scale as well as spatial relationships.

MANNERISM KEY FEATURES:

- illusion
- distortion of proportion
- inventive adaption of Classical elements
- adjusted rhythms of regularity
- emphasis of solid and void

SAN GIORGIO MAGGIORE, Venice, Italy, 1566–1610, Andrea Palladio, architect.

Only the pedimented white marble facade of this great church, dominated by four colossal Composite columns, is Mannerist; the interior is a traditional Christian church with a high central nave and two side aisles. Palladio's attempts to reconcile the facade with the central nave have produced an experiment in the combination of two temple fronts: one tall and slender, the other broader and lower. Superimposing one temple front on top of another has resulted in the broken lower pediment.

CHURCH OF THE GESÙ, Rome, Italy, 1568–80, Giacomo Barozzi da Vignola and Giacomo della Porta, architects.

The facade of this church, by della Porta, challenges Classical understanding of order and proportion. The facade is in two primary parts, upper and lower, joined by two upward-reaching volutes at either side and with a triangular pediment circumscribed by a round pediment seemingly bridging the overlapped space between the two sections.

SAINT JOHN'S CO-CATHEDRAL, Valletta, Malta, 1572–7, Girolamo Cassar, architect.

With a Mannerist facade, this church appears austere and fortress-like, with large, white columns supporting a speaking balcony above and empty niches to either side.

CHURCH OF MERCY, Tentugal, Coimbra, Portugal, sixteenth century, Tomé Velho and Francisco Rodrigues, architects.

The facade of this sixteenth-century church is considered of the Mannerist style. The most prominent element, the elongated sculptural portal, punctuates the roof line, splitting it in a similar way to a broken pediment.

VILLA FARNESE, Lazio, Italy, 1515–73, Antonio da Sangallo the Younger, Giacomo Barozzi da Vignola, and Baldassare Peruzzi, architects.

This villa, originally designed as a five-sided fortress-like structure, retains some of the mass of this idea, particularly with the large cube-like volumes located on the lower levels at each corner. The proportions on the facade break with ideals established in the Renaissance and feature double-height arched openings at the piano nobile, with three levels of small windows above.

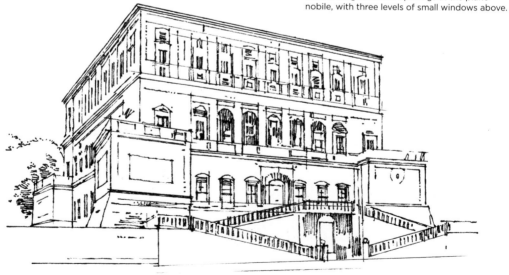

INTERNAL FACADE, Porta Pia, Rome, Italy, 1561–65, Michelangelo, architect.

The city-facing side of this gate in the Aurelian Walls of Rome is a confounding, mixed masterpiece of differences. With overscaled castellations, fragmented remnants of the orders, rustication, swags, pediments and multiple layered surfaces, among other attributes, the vocabulary of this gate defies principles of Classical order.

SAN GIOVANNI BATTISTA, Livorno, Tuscany, Italy, 1624, Giovanni Francesco Cantagallina, architect.

The facade of this church boasts several unique combinations of elements that challenge normative understanding of the combination of Classical elements. The oval window on the front is recessed and framed with a rectangle. The finely sculpted portal in marble sits in contrast to the plain facade with flat pilasters. And, lastly, the exaggerated rounded tympanum rises up in an unusual fashion from the entrance facade.

3

BAROQUE TO ART NOUVEAU

BAROQUE AND ROCOCO
SEVENTEENTH TO LATE EIGHTEENTH CENTURIES

The sweeping, highly articulated and dramatic forms of the Baroque style were a direct reaction to the stripped-down architectural attitudes generated through the Protestant Reformation in Europe. The papacy in Rome responded with exuberance, fuelling the development of this rich and theatrical style aimed at energizing and propagating the Catholic religion seated there. Featuring lavish pictorial ornamentation, a heightened play of light and shadow and dramatically decorated interiors, the origins of the term Baroque is debated – coming from Portuguese, Spanish or Italian – but relates to the idea of an irregular-shaped pearl. The term Baroque is seen as a negative commentary on the excessive architectural detailing of the style.

Rococo is considered to be an even more exuberant extension of Baroque and typically heightens Baroque excesses into a gilded, encrusted display of sumptuous materiality. The term Rococo is from the French word 'rocaille', which was used to describe the excessive shell-coated decorative work used in fabricated grottoes. The exorbitance of the Rococo style paved the way for the restraint of Neoclassicism.

BAROQUE AND ROCOCO KEY FEATURES:

- sweeping and/or curving forms
- concave and convex surfaces to mimic undulation
- exaggerated grandeur
- grand stairways
- use of the oval, both in plan and as ornament
- drama and contrast in lighting
- trompe-l'oeil treatments in interiors
- groupings of columns and niches
- twisting elements
- rich surface treatments
- giltwork, especially in Rococo

TREVI FOUNTAIN, Rome, Italy, 1732–62, Nicola Salvi, Giuseppe Pannini and others, architects.

The fountain is considered a late Baroque masterpiece. It features a central statue of Oceanus by Pietro Bracci, which is framed by a coffered semi-dome. The structure engages both Corinthian columns and pilasters rising up to a Baroque balustrade.

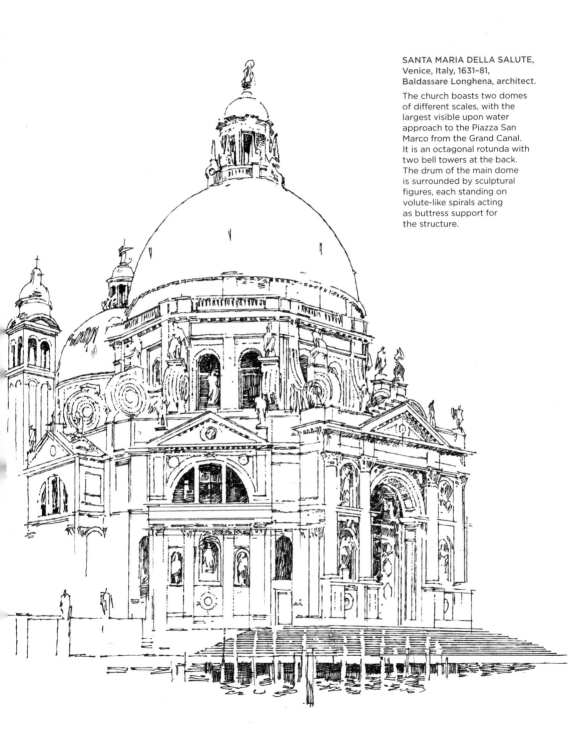

SANTA MARIA DELLA SALUTE,
Venice, Italy, 1631–81,
Baldassare Longhena, architect.

The church boasts two domes
of different scales, with the
largest visible upon water
approach to the Piazza San
Marco from the Grand Canal.
It is an octagonal rotunda with
two bell towers at the back.
The drum of the main dome
is surrounded by sculptural
figures, each standing on
volute-like spirals acting
as buttress support for
the structure.

SAN CARLO ALLE QUATTRO FONTANE, Rome, Italy, 1638–41, Francesco Borromini, architect.

The church features an undulating concave and convex facade emphasized through contrasting scaled columns. The crowning feature of an oval medallion – once boasting a fresco by Pietro Giarguzzi – is held aloft by supporting angels.

BAROQUE STAIR AT BOM JESUS DO MONTE, Braga, Portugal, 1781.

This monumental Baroque stairway is organized in a zigzag fashion as three stairways with associated terraces, and was constructed in three phases. The planes of the stairway are edged in contrasting stone surrounded by ornamental finials and figural sculpture.

CASA DE MATEUS, Vila Real, Portugal, 1739–43, Nicolau Nasoni, architect.

This Portuguese Baroque palace features a symmetrical entry within a courtyard enclosed by a low balustrade. The palace entrance is approached by way of a split scissor stair, topped with an ornamental pediment and flanked by two statuesque guards at the balustraded roof.

SANT'ANDREA AL QUIRINALE, Rome, Italy, 1658–70, Gian Lorenzo Bernini and Giovanni de'Rossi, architects.

The entry to the church proceeds up several steps and under a semicircular porch flanked with two Ionic columns. The facade is topped with a large pediment supported by Corinthian pilasters. Upon entry, the visitor moves quickly to the centre of the elliptical dome as the short axis faces the entrance and directly faces the high altar. The entire entrance sequence emphasizes the dramatic nature of the space.

CHÂTEAU DE MAISONS-LAFFITTE, near Paris, France, 1630–51, François Mansart, architect.

The château was an influential piece of French Baroque architecture, and features a front garden, large outer park and axial avenues connecting to the village and river.

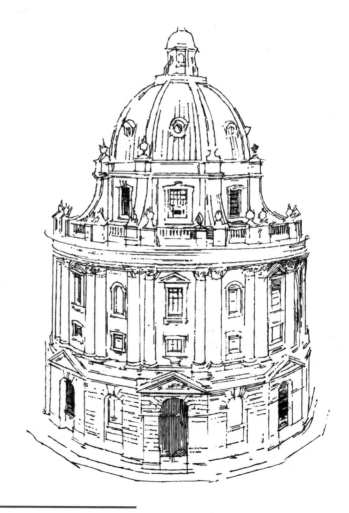

RADCLIFFE CAMERA, Oxford, England, 1737–48, James Gibbs, architect.

Considered English Baroque with elements of Palladianism, the Radcliffe Camera boasts the third largest dome in England, and is also considered the earliest example of a circular library in England.

ST PAUL'S CATHEDRAI,
London, England, 1675–1710,
Sir Christopher Wren, architect.

This English Baroque masterpiece rises above London and was the tallest structure in the city until 1963. The dome dominates the exterior and is actually two domes: an interior dome matching the scale of the inside of the cathedral, and an exterior dome rising above a drum of columns and niches. A brick cone resides in between the two and acts as an intervening structural element.

CHURCH OF ST JOHN OF NEPOMUK, Munich, Germany, 1733–46, Cosmas Damian Asam and Egid Quirin Asam, architects.

Considered a masterpiece of Bavarian Rococo, the church interior uses light and decoration to subdivide into three vertical zones, moving from darkness on the lower level to illuminated light expressed on the ceiling fresco.

SANTA SUSANNA, Rome, Italy, 1585–1603, Carlo Maderno, architect.

This Baroque facade is noted for the architectural illusion of height achieved through aligned Corinthian columns and vertical niches, as well as turned volutes reaching up towards the pediment.

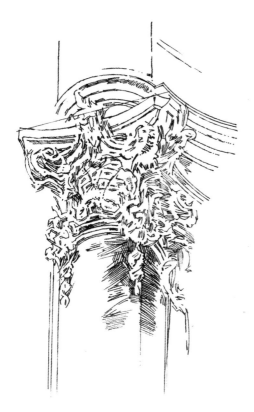

COLUMN CAPITAL, Engelszell Abbey, near
Engelhartszell an der Donau, Austria, 1754–64.

This interior Composite column is highly
ornamental and in the Rococo style.

ORNAMENTAL DECORATION, Helbling House,
Innsbruck, Austria, 1732, Anton Gigl, architect.

The elaborately detailed facade is Baroque, with
ornamental, stucco Rococo decorations added
in the eighteenth century.

CHINESE HOUSE, Sanssouci
Park, Potsdam, Germany,
1755–64, Johann Gottfried
Büring, architect.

Designed as a garden pavilion,
the Chinese House at Sanssouci
Park is in the chinoiserie style:
a mixture of traditional Chinese
architecture and Rococo
elements. The pavilion is in
a trefoil shape, with highly
decorative gilded columns and
a copper roof and cupola with
oval windows.

PALLADIANISM
EIGHTEENTH TO EARLY NINETEENTH CENTURIES

Strongly influenced by the sixteenth-century Venetian architect Andrea Palladio, Palladianism is inspired by Classical forms and characterized by symmetry and exacting proportion and order. Palladio retooled Classical architecture for contemporary practice and published these ideas in *The Four Books of Architecture* in 1570. The style was brought to England by Inigo Jones following his multiple trips to Italy in the early 1600s, and eventually took hold in England, Wales, Scotland, Ireland and North America.

PALLADIANISM KEY FEATURES:

- strict proportion
- symmetry
- displays Classical forms
- austere exteriors
- minimal ornament
- temple fronts

PALLADIAN BRIDGE, Prior Park, Bath, England, 1755, Richard Jones, architect.

The bridge is the primary visual highlight of this park landscape and features pediments at both entry points, as well as over the arches at the ends of the bridge length. Ionic columns rise above the balustrade and rusticated arches below.

CHISWICK HOUSE, London, England, 1726–29, Richard Boyle and William Kent, architects.

Chiswick House is a Palladian villa designed as a simpler, symmetrical structure based on the classic Palladio-designed Villa Capra, as well as other masterpieces of Rome. Unique features include a steep-pitched dome in an octagonal form, six Corinthian columns on the portico sitting above a rusticated stone base, Palladian windows and a split stairway grand entrance.

PALLADIAN BRIDGE, Stowe Gardens, Stowe, England, 1738, James Gibbs, architect.

This view of the pedimented bridge entrance with balustrade surround shows the top of the entrance arch, featuring a sculpted face as the ornamental keystone.

STOWE HOUSE, Stowe, England, 1677–1779.

This view of the north facade rises up from the lawn with a modified monumental stair to a portico entrance. It is modest in decoration and largely symmetrical, as are the other facades of the house. The portico is supported by four Ionic columns with two Ionic pilasters and limited decoration other than a band of dentils on the tympanum of the pediment. The exterior of the house has not been significantly altered since its completion in 1779.

MEREWORTH CASTLE, Kent, England, 1723–25, Colen Campbell, architect.

This building demonstrates the firm symmetrical relationship of spaces, moving from one portico porch through the central dome space and out to the opposite portico porch.

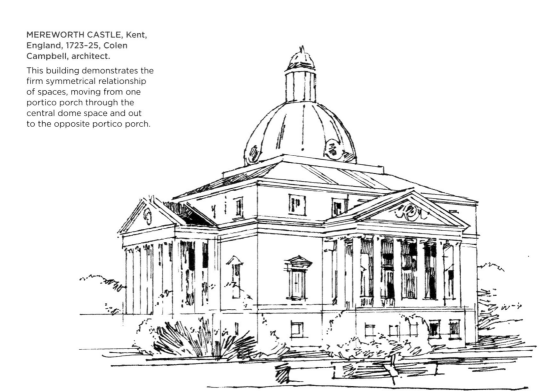

HOLBURNE MUSEUM, Bath, England, 1796–99, Charles Harcourt Masters, architect.

The entrance to the museum is on axis with the garden, but instead of rising up to the portico porch, the entrance is underneath, nestled within a series of three arches. The porch acts as a marker of the entry but is not the entrance itself; instead it is a spatial extension from the main room of the piano nobile into the covered space of the portico.

BERLIN STATE OPERA HOUSE, Berlin, Germany, 1741–1843, Georg Wenzeslaus von Knobelsdorff, Carl Gotthard Langhans and Carl Ferdinand Langhans, architects.

Familiar to Palladian architecture, the split scissor stair rises up to a portico entrance and forces a side entry and then reorientation to the actual entrance of the building. This particular pediment features a sculpted tympanum lined with dentils and prominent figural sculptures rising above.

WANSTED HOUSE, London, England, 1715–22 (demolished in 1825), Colen Campbell, architect.

This drawing demonstrates the symmetry and order of Palladian architecture. The house features a split scissor stair rising up to an elevated portico with a classic temple front.

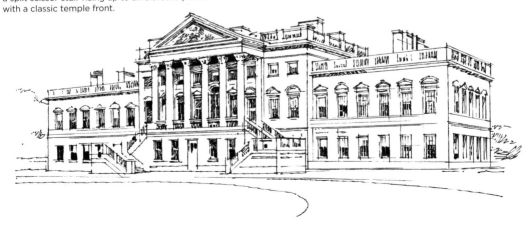

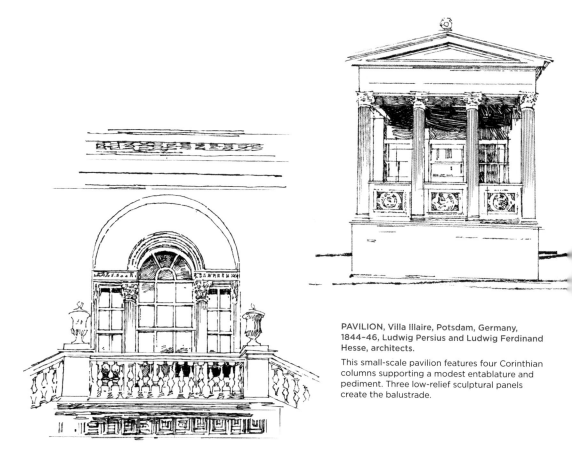

PAVILION, Villa Illaire, Potsdam, Germany, 1844–46, Ludwig Persius and Ludwig Ferdinand Hesse, architects.

This small-scale pavilion features four Corinthian columns supporting a modest entablature and pediment. Three low-relief sculptural panels create the balustrade.

PALLADIAN WINDOW, Chiswick House, London, England, 1726–29, Richard Boyle and William Kent, architects.

A Palladian window is a three-part window with a large, arched centre window flanked by narrow openings on each side, typically with a flat lintel above.

HOLKHAM HALL, Holkham, England, 1734–64, Thomas Coke, Matthew Brettingham and William Kent, architects.

This country house is fully symmetrical in elevation and plan, featuring a central block of primary rooms with four identical and symmetrical wings radiating from each corner.

KEDLESTON HALL, Kedleston, England, 1759–65, James Paine, Matthew Brettingham and Robert Adam, architects.

The south facade pictured was designed by Robert Adam, based on the Arch of Constantine in Rome. The entrance is surrounded by four engaged Corinthian columns topped with figural sculpture and an embellished cornice acting as a parapet. The northern (front) facade is pure Palladianism, with a pedimented portico and statues at the apex.

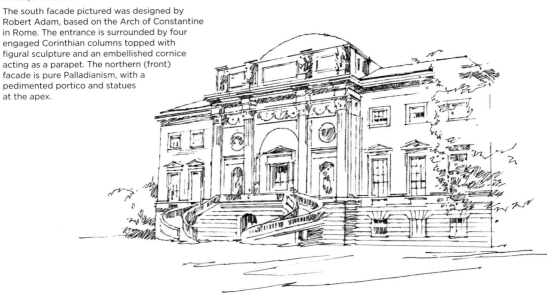

HOUGHTON HALL, Houghton, England, 1722–29, Colen Campbell, James Gibbs and William Kent, architects.

The engaged columns and flattened pediment on the facade of this grand country house mark the entry at the piano nobile but do not create a covered porch. Instead, two sets of symmetrical straight stairs rise up to a patio at the entrance. On either side of the entrance pediment are two fine examples of Palladian windows.

GEORGIAN

1714–1830

The Georgian style was particularly prevalent in English-speaking countries, and is characterized by symmetry, proportion and balance. Ornament in this style is restrained – sometimes not even evident on the exterior of a building – and was based on Classical Roman and Greek architecture. The name is derived from its time period in England, where the British monarchs were George I, George II, George III and George IV from the House of Hanover. Throughout its term, the Georgian style influenced residences, public buildings and churches. Of note was the abundant development of terraced housing, as the period coincided with a time of great economic prosperity.

GEORGIAN KEY FEATURES:

- axial symmetry
- facade symmetry
- flatter, stepped facades
- townhouses
- urbanist housing known as terraced housing
- minimal ornament
- sash windows
- Classical proportions
- constructed with brick or stone and often with stone quoins

BEDFORD SQUARE, London, England, 1775–83, Thomas Leverton, architect.

An early example of Georgian terraced housing, the facades at Bedford Square are repetitive and modest, with blocked stone arches marking individual entrances. Terraced housing is often three storeys, as this example demonstrates.

ST GEORGE'S, Bloomsbury, England, 1716–31, Nicholas Hawksmoor, architect.

It doesn't get more Georgian than a statue of King George I in Roman dress perched atop the stepped tower of this church! Hawksmoor put his eccentric attitude on full display by adding two lions and two unicorns at the base of the tower, one on each corner. Instead of standing in a regal pose, the four animals appear to be playing with one another.

APSLEY HOUSE, London, England, 1771–78, Robert Adam, architect.

Originally built in red brick, the house was clad in Bath stone and the pediment added in 1819 by architect Benjamin Dean Wyatt. The pedimented porch is shallow and dominated by four Corinthian columns. The house facade is flat, with no ornament surrounding the sash windows, and steps back with Corinthian pilasters at each turning edge.

ROYAL CRESCENT, Bath, England, 1767–74, John Wood, the Younger, architect.

A fine example of Georgian urbanism, the Royal Crescent in Bath is a single row of thirty terraced houses laid out in a symmetrical, curved crescent. The facade remains largely unchanged and includes 114 engaged Ionic columns at the second level above a rusticated ground floor.

CARLYLE HOUSE, Alexandria, Virginia, US, 1751–53, John Carlyle, architect.

The front door to the house is surrounded by blocked stone with an enlarged keystone above the rounded transom window. Transom windows were used for both privacy and ventilation.

ISAAC MEASON HOUSE IN DUNBAR TOWNSHIP, Pennsylvania, US, 1802, Isaac Meason and Adam Wilson, architects.

The Isaac Meason House is a typical example of Georgian architecture in the United States. The sandstone facade with an ashlar finish falls largely in one plane, with a symmetrical pediment marking the central entry to the home. The central facade is flanked by symmetrical single-storey wings on each side.

SIR JOHN SOANE'S MUSEUM, London, England, 1808–9, Sir John Soane, architect.

Soane designed this house, now a museum, by combining three adjacent homes. As a professor of architecture, Soane was known for his innovative use of light and experimentation with Classical forms. The projecting stone facade was added by Soane in 1812 and shows significant symmetry and restraint of ornament.

CHRIST CHURCH, Spitalfields, London, England, 1714–29, Nicholas Hawksmoor, architect.

The predominant architectural feature at the entrance to this church is the monumental arched pediment at the entry portico, supported by four Tuscan columns resting on overscaled pedestals. The plan of the church is a simple rectangle that extrudes into a three-tiered tower with elongated and exaggerated steeple, actively extending the visual impact of the arched pediment of the entrance below.

WILLIAM MORRIS GALLERY (formerly Water House), London, England, 1744–50.

Once the Morris family home, this museum is dedicated to William Morris, the English Arts and Crafts designer. The semicircular bays along with horizontal banding and upper cornice were added in the late eighteenth century in a bid to merge with the Georgian elements of the original facade at the centre. The front porch is framed with fluted Corinthian columns carved of wood.

MARBLE HILL HOUSE, Twickenham, England, 1724–29, Roger Morris and Henry Herbert, architects.

The house has a compact and modest geometric plan and a restrained facade typical of Georgian houses. The north facade pictured emphasizes the piano nobile, with a rusticated base directly underneath the engaged portico, supported by Ionic pilasters. The windows at the main level are topped with either modest architraves – horizontal bands that extend beyond the window edges – or a simple pediment.

CLASSICAL REVIVAL
MID-EIGHTEENTH TO MID-NINETEENTH CENTURIES

The simplified buildings of the Classical Revival were largely a response to the audacity and extremes of the Baroque and Rococo styles, as were Palladianism, Georgian and other Neoclassical styles. The difference was that proponents of the Classical Revival looked directly at the architecture of Ancient Rome and Ancient Greece rather than emulating existing interpretations of those styles. Scottish architect Robert Adam was one of the central designers of the Classical Revival and believed that gaining first-hand knowledge from remains of antiquity was invaluable to the understanding of architecture. He spent significant time in Italy studying with Charles-Louis Clérisseau, a French draughtsman and antiquarian, and Giovanni Battista Piranesi, an Italian artist specializing in representation of ancient architecture. Upon his return, Adam published his book *Ruins of the Palace of the Emperor Diocletian at Spalatro in Dalmatia,* establishing himself as an expert..

CLASSICAL REVIVAL KEY FEATURES:

- Classical proportions
- Classical ornament
- significant use of columns
- monumentality
- symmetry
- design purity
- repetition of elements

ARC DE TRIOMPHE, Paris, France, 1806–36, Jean-François-Thérèse Chalgrin, architect.

This monumental, triumphal arch stands at the end of the Champs-Élysées and is a significant urban organizer, forming a plaza at the intersection of twelve radiating avenues in Paris. The commemorative monument celebrates military achievements and features a coffered barrel vault, four pillars adorned with large sculptural reliefs and a hefty, ornamental cornice.

**THE ROTUNDA, University
of Virginia, Charlottesville,
Virginia, US, 1822–26, Thomas
Jefferson, architect.**

Modelled after the style and
proportions of the Pantheon in
Rome, the Rotunda is superbly
symmetrical with a large,
prominent pedimented portico,
with Corinthian columns and
decorative dentils lining the
pediment and extending around
the drum of the central dome.

**FOUR COURTS, Dublin, Ireland, 1786–1802,
Thomas Cooley and James Gandon, architects.**

The Four Courts building is dominated by
a copper dome sitting above a dramatic and
elongated drum, encircled with thin columns.
The primary building mass is symmetrical and
fronted with a columned portico with pediment.
Figural sculptures reach into the sky above the
balustraded cornice.

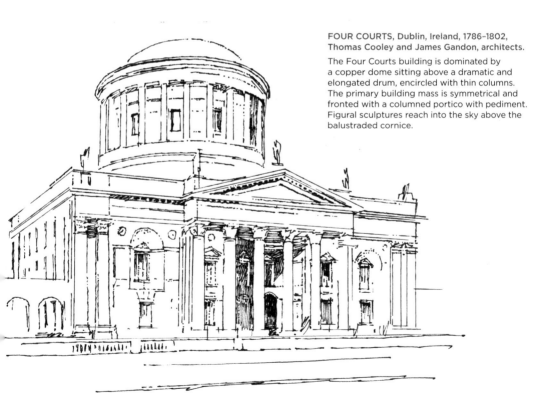

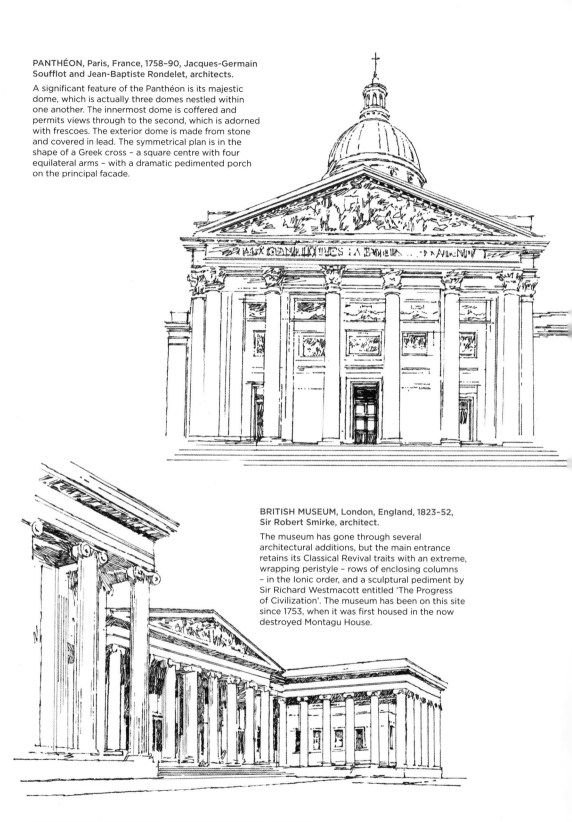

PANTHÉON, Paris, France, 1758–90, Jacques-Germain Soufflot and Jean-Baptiste Rondelet, architects.

A significant feature of the Panthéon is its majestic dome, which is actually three domes nestled within one another. The innermost dome is coffered and permits views through to the second, which is adorned with frescoes. The exterior dome is made from stone and covered in lead. The symmetrical plan is in the shape of a Greek cross – a square centre with four equilateral arms – with a dramatic pedimented porch on the principal facade.

BRITISH MUSEUM, London, England, 1823–52, Sir Robert Smirke, architect.

The museum has gone through several architectural additions, but the main entrance retains its Classical Revival traits with an extreme, wrapping peristyle – rows of enclosing columns – in the Ionic order, and a sculptural pediment by Sir Richard Westmacott entitled 'The Progress of Civilization'. The museum has been on this site since 1753, when it was first housed in the now destroyed Montagu House.

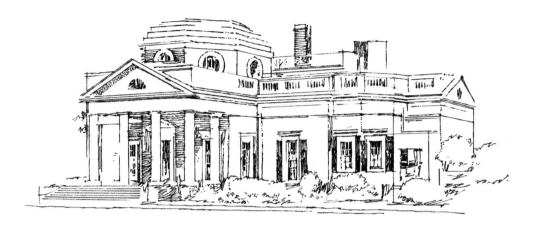

MONTICELLO, Charlottesville, Virginia, US, 1769–1809, Thomas Jefferson, architect.

The house is considered to be Jefferson's masterpiece and was built over forty years as he continued to enlarge and remodel it. Jefferson designed the brick home to have multiple fronts, reflected in the duelling pedimented porticos. The entablature of each pediment reaches around the entire structure and supports a balustrade that visually connects the two fronts.

BRANDENBURG GATE, Berlin, Germany, 1788–91, Carl Gotthard Langhans, architect.

This monumental gate was one of eighteen gates surrounding the old fortified city and neighbouring suburbs. Its proportions are similar to that of a triumphal arch, albeit without the arch. There are twelve engaged Doric columns, six on each side, joined by thick walls standing perpendicular to the face of the gate, creating five entryways. There is a stepped stone element on the face of the cornice that directs the eye up towards the Quadriga statue, depicting the goddess of victory driving a horse-drawn chariot.

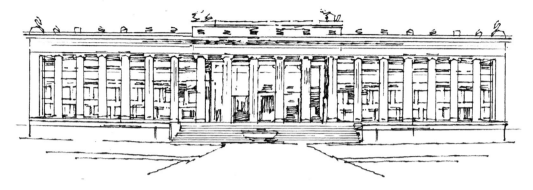

ALTES MUSEUM, Berlin, Germany, 1823–30,
Karl Friedrich Schinkel, architect.

The extreme length of the museum facade is
accentuated by the grand row of eighteen Ionic
columns enclosing the portico and rising up
from the monumental entry stair. The building is
rectangular and contains two courtyards flanking
a central rotunda with a coffered interior dome.

BANK OF ENGLAND, London, England,
1788–1833, Sir John Soane, architect.

The large, urban scale of this building – spanning
an entire city block – is fortress-like on the street
level, with some facades solid block and others
elongated through multiple repetitive columns.
The building breaks down its monumentality
by stepping the facade back to the occupiable
core. Several different porticos punctuate these
recessed upper levels. On this particular facade,
the raised pedimented portico is framed with
a series of paired, Composite columns. The
building was largely rebuilt by Herbert Baker
from 1921–42.

KONZERTHAUS BERLIN, Berlin, Germany, 1818–21, Karl Friedrich Schinkel, architect.

Although the theatre was damaged significantly during the war, Schinkel's core structure and exterior remain. The building extends upwards with great monumentality, owing in large part to the staircase, Ionic columns of the portico, and the double pediments visible on both the front portico and the building mass beyond. Schinkel deliberately divided the core structure into three primary parts: the central section was the large theatre, with one wing serving as rehearsal halls and the other as the smaller concert hall.

HELSINKI CATHEDRAL, Helsinki, Finland, 1830–52, Carl Ludvig Engel, architect.

The cathedral sits on an elevated plinth accessible by way of a grand, monumental stairway. The expression of height is further accentuated by the tall dome supported by an elongated drum with engaged columns. This central dome is surrounded by four smaller domes. The cathedral was originally built to honour Russian Tsar Nicholas I and was based on the design of St Isaac's Cathedral of St Petersburg.

GOTHIC REVIVAL
LATE EIGHTEENTH TO EARLY TWENTIETH CENTURIES

As a departure from the Classical styles of the time, the Gothic Revival movement sought to return to the lost traditions of Medieval architecture. At the centre of the movement were three architectural theorists: A. W. N. Pugin, John Ruskin and Eugène Viollet-le-Duc. Pugin argued that a return to a Gothic style would precipitate a return to the morality of the Medieval religious world. Ruskin did not agree and felt that it would provide a rich opportunity for craftsmen to regain autonomy over their craft. Viollet-le-Duc, on the other hand, felt the qualities of materials of the Gothic style and their intrinsic structural properties were reason enough to return to the style.

Gothic Revival is characterized by lavishly decorated interiors and exteriors with pointed arches, quatrefoil windows, leaded glass, steep roofs, thin spires, grouped chimneys and shaped parapets, and is quite clearly a revival of the Gothic style.

GOTHIC REVIVAL KEY FEATURES:

- pointed arches
- steep-pitched roofs
- thin spires
- multifoil ornament
- leaded glass
- elements to emphasize verticality

ROYAL COURTS OF JUSTICE, London, England, 1866–82, George Edmund Street, architect.

Street won this commission by way of an architectural design competition in 1867. Though the building looks like a Gothic cathedral, it was designed for the courts from inception. The exterior references Gothic architecture with a recessed pointed arch entry, rows of trefoil pointed arches, a large central rose window, lancet windows and Gothic spires.

SINT-PETRUS-EN-PAULUSKERK, Ostend, Belgium, 1899–1908, Louis Delacenserie, architect.

The monumental entrance facade sports numerous elements indicative of Gothic Revival architecture. The entrance is framed by a stepped archivolt – profiled decoration inside an arch – and is topped by a shaped ogee arch. The primary entrance is formally mimicked by two side entrances at a smaller scale. The rose window dominates the centre of the primary facade, with multiple pinnacles topped with vegetative – flowers, buds or curled leaves – ornaments.

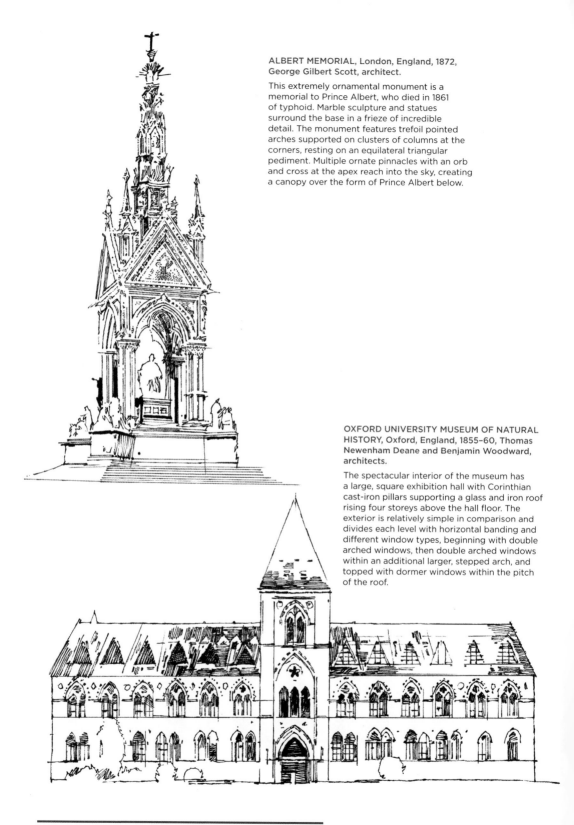

ALBERT MEMORIAL, London, England, 1872, George Gilbert Scott, architect.

This extremely ornamental monument is a memorial to Prince Albert, who died in 1861 of typhoid. Marble sculpture and statues surround the base in a frieze of incredible detail. The monument features trefoil pointed arches supported on clusters of columns at the corners, resting on an equilateral triangular pediment. Multiple ornate pinnacles with an orb and cross at the apex reach into the sky, creating a canopy over the form of Prince Albert below.

OXFORD UNIVERSITY MUSEUM OF NATURAL HISTORY, Oxford, England, 1855–60, Thomas Newenham Deane and Benjamin Woodward, architects.

The spectacular interior of the museum has a large, square exhibition hall with Corinthian cast-iron pillars supporting a glass and iron roof rising four storeys above the hall floor. The exterior is relatively simple in comparison and divides each level with horizontal banding and different window types, beginning with double arched windows, then double arched windows within an additional larger, stepped arch, and topped with dormer windows within the pitch of the roof.

WOOLWORTH BUILDING, New York City, New York, US, 1910–12, Cass Gilbert, architect.

The top pyramidal tower of the Woolworth Building caps the skyscraper and sits on a stepped tower with pinnacles accentuating the corners. Each step in the facade as the building rises upwards is framed with ogee arched skirts that frame each of the windows below.

TRINITY CHURCH, New York City, New York, US, 1839–46, Richard Upjohn, architect.

Richard Upjohn was considered one of the leaders of the Gothic Revival movement in the United States, and as such this church relies on multiple architectural features to support its designation. It is embellished with Gothic spires, pinnacles and pointed arches. The main spire is magnificent in proportion to the primary form of the church.

THE GALLERY, Strawberry Hill House, London, England, 1747–90, Horace Walpole, architect.

The Gallery is one of the most spectacular interiors of the house, featuring elaborate, gilded fan vaulting made entirely of papier mâché.

MANCHESTER TOWN HALL, Manchester, England, 1868–77, Alfred Waterhouse, architect.

This municipal building displays limited carved decoration but still manages to express the lightness of Gothic Revival structures through its window detailing, horizontal banding and multiple scaled pinnacles at the roof edge surrounding the prominent central clock tower.

DUKE UNIVERSITY CHAPEL, Durham, North Carolina, US, 1930–32, Julian F. Abele and Horace Trumbauer, architects.

The chapel is in a crucifix form with pointed arches, rib vaulting and an impressive roof line with surrounding pinnacles. It was built in the Collegiate Gothic style – a subset of Gothic Revival particular to high schools and universities in the United States.

VOTIVKIRCHE, Vienna, Austria, 1856–79, Heinrich von Ferstel, architect.

The Votivkirche facade stands flanked by two slim towers flush with Gothic pinnacles. The tower tops are distinct, with patterned tiling on their roofs. There are three entrances, all with archivolts, just below the central rose window.

ST GILES CATHOLIC CHURCH, Cheadle, England, 1841–46, Augustus Welby Northmore Pugin, architect.

The extraordinarily patterned and painted interior of the church belies its austere exterior. The altar end has a massive Gothic window with stone tracery. The main church spire rises up above the roof line with multiple lancet windows, pinnacles and spires.

EXOTIC REVIVAL
LATE EIGHTEENTH TO MID-TWENTIETH CENTURIES

The Exotic Revival style is characterized as a Western reproduction of certain aspects of Eastern architecture and includes many different cultures in its evolution. Egyptian, Indian, Moorish, Chinese and even Mayan civilizations had a profound architectural influence on buildings during this time. The interaction between Eastern and Western cultures, and the subsequent interest in the development of this style, was largely influenced through colonization.

EXOTIC REVIVAL KEY FEATURES:

- onion domes
- ogee and horseshoe arches
- minarets
- Egyptian motifs: palm or lotus capitals, winged discs
- replicas of traditional cultural buildings

DOMES AND MINARETS, Royal Pavilion, Brighton, England, 1815–23, John Nash, architect.

The Royal Pavilion was designed in an Indo-Gothic style and underwent four different building phases. The front is organized in five parts, with a central, focal colonnaded rotunda. The onion dome is supported by a cast- and wrought-iron frame located inside the structure. It is topped by an ornamental finial and flanked by two minarets.

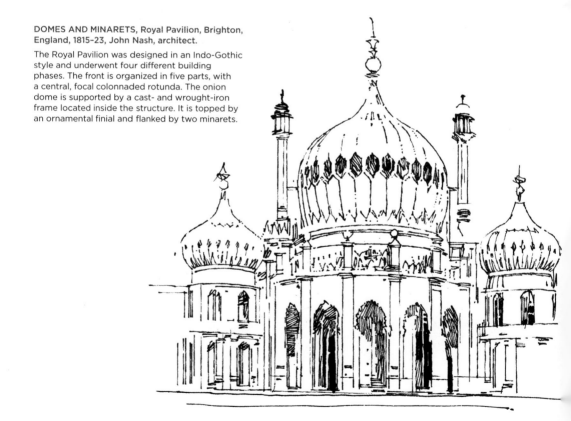

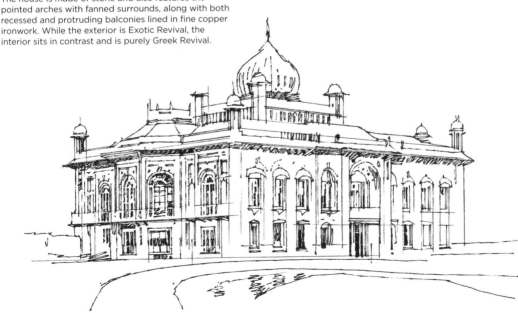

VORONTSOV PALACE, Alupka, Crimea, 1828–48, Edward Blore and William Hunt, architects.

There are distinct style differences on the primary facades of the palace. On the northern entrance facade pictured, the style is a mix of ancient fortified structure and Indo-Gothic, with the heavy stonework combined with pinnacles and shortened, structured onion domes. The southern facade continues with the Indo-Gothic theme but is much lighter, with less stonework and more carved stone screens.

SEZINCOTE HOUSE, Gloucestershire, England, 1805, Samuel Pepys Cockerell, architect.

This grand Mughal-Indian Revival home is topped with a copper onion dome and reaches into the countryside via a long, curved, arcaded structure that features pointed arches with fanned carving for the surround. The house is made of stone and also features the pointed arches with fanned surrounds, along with both recessed and protruding balconies lined in fine copper ironwork. While the exterior is Exotic Revival, the interior sits in contrast and is purely Greek Revival.

RED MOSQUE, Schwetzingen Palace, Schwetzingen, Germany, 1779–95, Nicolas de Pigage, architect.

Located in the garden of the palace, this folly served as an indication of the enlightenment and cosmopolitan nature of the palace owners. Designed in an Islamic style, it consists of a domed building, two minarets and a spectacular arcade lined with trefoil ogee arches.

IRANISTAN, Bridgeport, Connecticut, US, 1848, Leopold Eidlitz, architect.

Iranistan was the home of P. T. Barnum, a famed American circus showman, and was designed in a mix of Turkish, Moorish and Byzantine styles. The house burned down in 1857 and was completely destroyed. Symmetrical in design, it boasted multiple onion domes, pinnacles and porches topped with arched carved screens.

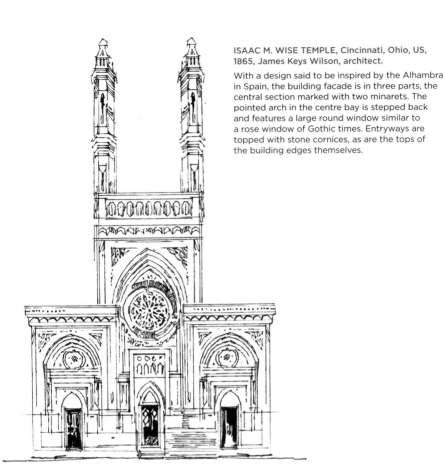

ISAAC M. WISE TEMPLE, Cincinnati, Ohio, US, 1865, James Keys Wilson, architect.

With a design said to be inspired by the Alhambra in Spain, the building facade is in three parts, the central section marked with two minarets. The pointed arch in the centre bay is stepped back and features a large round window similar to a rose window of Gothic times. Entryways are topped with stone cornices, as are the tops of the building edges themselves.

GEORGIAN NATIONAL OPERA THEATRE, Tbilisi, Georgia, 1896, Viktor Schröter, architect.

The theatre was designed in clear Moorish Revival style, with strong horizontal banding on the exterior. The entrance is marked by a large pointed arch decorated with fine sculpted scrollwork, revealing an elevated porch that frames the entry.

CORN PALACE, Mitchell, South Dakota, US, 1891–1921, Rapp and Rapp, architects.

The Corn Palace – named due to its cladding in various designs made entirely of corn, which are redesigned and replaced every year by local artists – is a midwestern folk art destination designed in the Moorish Revival style. The domes and minarets were added in 1937. The building serves as a community venue for a variety of events.

FORUM, Melbourne, Australia, 1929, John Eberson and Bohringer, Taylor & Johnson, architects.

Designed as an atmospheric theatre – the interior is intended to look like a walled garden – the building has a Moorish Revival exterior with minarets, and a tall, domed clock tower marking the corner of the building in its urban setting. The facade is highly articulated carved stone with small balconies and porches subtly embedded in the surface.

ARAB HALL, Leighton House Museum, Holland Park, London, England, 1877–79, George Aitchison, architect.

While construction on the house began as early as 1866, work on the design and construction of the Arab Hall did not begin until 1877 and occurred directly after Leighton, the homeowner, made trips to Turkey, Egypt and Syria. With detailed mosaics, walls covered in Islamic tiles and a gold dome, the resplendent room is said to be modelled directly on a twelfth-century palace called La Zisa, located in Palermo, Italy.

GREAT PAGODA, Kew Gardens, London, England, 1757–62, William Chambers, architect.

This pagoda was considered to be a Chinese-inspired garden folly, one of several buildings designed by Chambers at Kew. The pagoda has ten octagonal storeys, each rising up in a tapered fashion, and provides stunning views of both the garden and the city.

CHINESISCHER TURM (Chinese Tower), Englischer Garten, Munich, Germany, 1789–90, Joseph Frey, architect.

An 25-m-high (82 ft) wooden structure, the Chinese Tower was modelled on the much taller Great Pagoda in Kew Gardens, England. This particular structure was damaged during the war and rebuilt to the exact same specifications in the mid-twentieth century. It now serves as one of Munich's largest public beer gardens.

ALMAS TEMPLE, Washington, DC, US, 1929, Allen Hussell Potts, architect.

Colourful, terracotta tile patterns are arrayed on the facade of this Masonic Temple with strong Moorish influences. The central portal is highly decorated with a crenellated top, levels of multi-scaled arches, framed in an intricate geometric pattern with a recessed entrance under monumental Moorish arches.

FOX THEATRE, Atlanta, Georgia, US, 1928–29, Marye, Alger & Vinour, architects.

Originally designed as the Yaarab Shrine Temple – headquarters of the Shriners organization – the project ran out of funding and was leased to movie production executive William Fox; it opened in 1929 as a movie theatre. The building's nod to Exotic Revival comes in two primary styles: Islamic and Egyptian. The most spectacular space is the auditorium, which replicates an Arabian courtyard with a night sky of twinkling lights, a surround of castle walls and is topped with a replica of a Bedouin tent that actually acts as part of the air-conditioning system. All surfaces within the theatre are painted and glazed plaster; nothing is as it seems!

OLD EGYPTIAN COURTHOUSE (now a warehouse), New Orleans, Louisiana, US, 1843, James Gallier, architect.

Originally serving as a courthouse for small town Lafayette, the building is a clear example of Egyptian Revival. Though no longer retaining all of its original Egyptian mouldings, it still maintains its massive presence and tapered entry points topped with abstracted winged scarabs.

CONGREGATION RODEPH SHALOM, Philadelphia, Pennsylvania, US, 1866, Frank Furness, architect.

This synagogue building is designed in a Byzantine Revival style and features a limestone-clad exterior and lush interior with mosaics, patterned marble flooring and painted decorative stencilling. The entrance is marked by three overscaled, elongated semicircular arches, each with patterned giltwork as a highlight beneath.

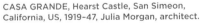

CASA GRANDE, Hearst Castle, San Simeon, California, US, 1919–47, Julia Morgan, architect.

The design of the main house at the Hearst Castle is in the Spanish Revival style – a particular subset of Exotic Revival popular in California at the time – and is an exuberant mix of multiple architectural styles and cultures including Baroque and Rococo, with Mediterranean influences. The structure is cast in concrete with stone cladding on the facade.

BEAUX ARTS
LATE NINETEENTH TO EARLY TWENTIETH CENTURIES

The Beaux Arts style was named after the École des Beaux-Arts in Paris and was seen as an eclectic and resplendent mix of Greek, Roman, Gothic, Renaissance and Baroque architectural elements. It introduced widespread use of the modern materials of iron and glass, and was considered to be a veritable French architectural style. Often utilizing layered facades rich with adornment, the Beaux Arts style was largely implemented through the design of grand civic buildings.

BEAUX ARTS KEY FEATURES:

- grand civic buildings
- layered facades
- Classical elements
- sculptural pieces, especially at the roof line
- high, monumental facades
- rusticated bases
- columned piano nobile
- rich sculptural adornments
- iron structures

MUSÉE D'ORSAY, Paris, France, 1898–1900, Victor Laloux, architect.

Originally designed and built as a railway station, this museum in Paris sits majestically on the Left Bank of the Seine. Large glass and iron barrel vaults dominate the roof line and illuminate the great interior hall that references its days as a train station in its grand length and height. The limestone facade features seven monumental arched entries flanked by two large clock towers, and is embellished with multiple sculptures and an impressive French mansard roof.

ST JAMES BUILDING, New York City, New York, US, 1898, Bruce Price, architect.

This sixteen-storey steel-framed building, now an office building but originally a hotel, has a limestone base and a limestone capital with a large brick shaft in between. This elaborate window assembly is in the upper capital portion of the building. It has lionhead brackets supporting engaged modified Composite columns with a semicircular arch above, all highly articulated with carved limestone ornamental embellishments. The window has a pedimented top above a dentiled entablature resplendent with acroteria at the apex and corners.

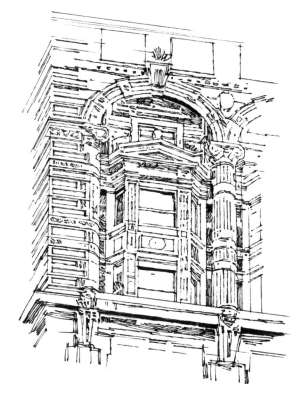

PALAIS GARNIER, Paris, France, 1861–75, Charles Garnier, architect.

Aside from its literary fame – this opera house was used as the setting for Gaston Leroux's novel *The Phantom of the Opera* – the building is a great example of a Beaux Arts civic building. The ground entry level is rusticated with ornamental roundels between arches. The piano nobile is lined in column pairs with recessed panels sporting windows, and a secondary set of smaller columns. The roof is topped with an exaggerated and splendidly carved cornice topped with gilded sculptures and a low, elliptical dome above.

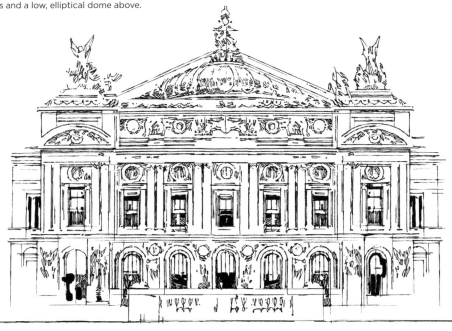

CATHEDRAL OF ST PAUL, St Paul, Minnesota, US, 1906–15, Emmanuel Louis Masqueray, architect.

With a Greek cross as the plan, the exterior of the church is dominated by a central dome, surrounded in pilasters topped by pinnacles. The large stone edifice at the entrance features a semicircular arch with an embedded rose window and highly carved gable above, flanked by two square towers. The cross plan allows for unobstructed views inside the church, revealing the pulpit and the altar.

PETIT PALAIS, Paris, France, 1897–1900, Charles Girault, architect.

The Petit Palais is a clear example of the use of an imbricated facade, which steps forward and back and appears layered with Classical elements. In this particular case, the line of columns at the piano nobile with the secondary facade behind exemplifies this idea. The entrance extends even further forward to receive visitors under a magnificent layered arch surrounded by engaged columns, topped with a dome and ornate cupola.

GRAND CENTRAL TERMINAL, New York City, New York, US, 1903–13, Reed and Stern, Warren and Wetmore, architects.

As one of the world's largest train stations, Grand Central Terminal has forty-four platforms. The monumental exterior expresses the Beaux Arts style that swept through New York at the turn of the century, gaining traction as part of the City Beautiful movement, the premise of which was that well-designed and distinguished architecture would support civic pride and therefore social order. The main facade of the station has a monumental clock that is the world's largest example of Tiffany glass, with a sculptural surround.

CAROLANDS CHATEAU, Hillsborough, California, US, 1914–16, Ernest Sanson, architect.

Designed with clear inspiration from François Mansart, this home celebrates the French mansard roof – steep sides and a double pitch – with two peaked mansards with a central dome above the main entrance. Rectangular and circular dormer windows punctuate the roof at regular and symmetrical intervals.

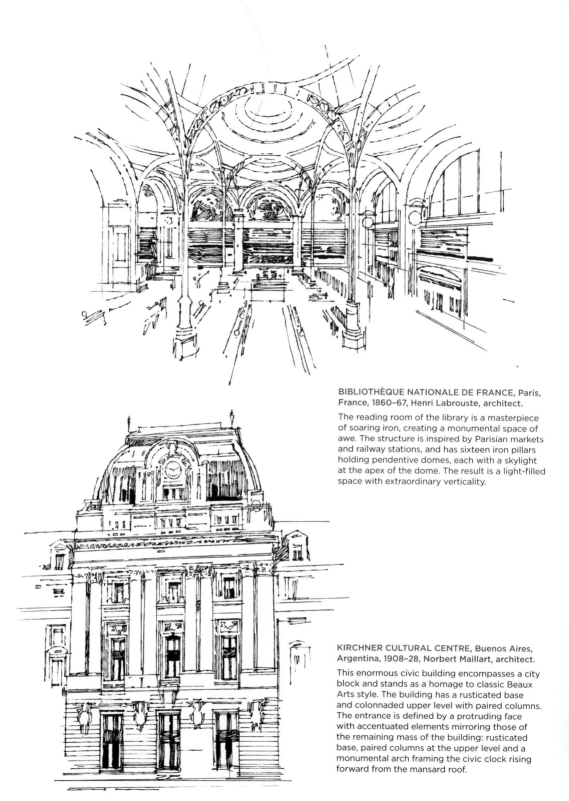

BIBLIOTHÈQUE NATIONALE DE FRANCE, Paris, France, 1860–67, Henri Labrouste, architect.

The reading room of the library is a masterpiece of soaring iron, creating a monumental space of awe. The structure is inspired by Parisian markets and railway stations, and has sixteen iron pillars holding pendentive domes, each with a skylight at the apex of the dome. The result is a light-filled space with extraordinary verticality.

KIRCHNER CULTURAL CENTRE, Buenos Aires, Argentina, 1908–28, Norbert Maillart, architect.

This enormous civic building encompasses a city block and stands as a homage to classic Beaux Arts style. The building has a rusticated base and colonnaded upper level with paired columns. The entrance is defined by a protruding face with accentuated elements mirroring those of the remaining mass of the building: rusticated base, paired columns at the upper level and a monumental arch framing the civic clock rising forward from the mansard roof.

FIFTH AVENUE FACADE, Metropolitan Museum of Art, New York City, New York, US, 1902, Richard Morris Hunt, architect.

The Beaux Arts facade facing Fifth Avenue was an addition to the ill-received Victorian Gothic style of the original design. This primary entrance is reached by ascending a monumental stair and entering the centre of three semicircular arches with ornamental keystones. The arches are embedded within a series of paired Corinthian columns. Atop the columns is an exaggerated cornice rife with acroteria at regular intervals.

PONT ALEXANDRE III, Paris, France, 1896–1900, Joseph Cassien-Bernard and Gaston Cousin, architects.

This Beaux Arts bridge extends across the River Seine with a single-span steel arch – considered to be a significant achievement of nineteenth-century engineering. The arch of the bridge is decorated with stone swags and sculptural heads. It combines styles, with the addition of Art Nouveau lanterns flanked by cherubs along with other sculptures reminiscent of this additional style.

ARTS AND CRAFTS
LATE NINETEENTH TO EARLY TWENTIETH CENTURIES

The primary tenet of the Arts and Crafts movement was to create an architectural style that expressed the hand of the craftsman who created it. The style acted in direct opposition to the industrialization and mechanization of the world – both seen as conditions of impending modernity. The Arts and Crafts style was most widely experimented with in domestic architecture, and embraced such elements as exposed beams, crafted woodwork and picturesque connections to nature.

RED HOUSE, Bexleyheath, London, England, 1859–60, Philip Webb and Richard Morris, architects.

This house celebrates vernacular charm. Built to eschew the industrial nature of society, the home focuses on the revival of the exaltation of the work of individual craftsmen that was necessary during Medieval times. As a nod to the Medieval architecture, the home has steeply pitched roofs with multiple chimneys. Built in red brick, the home gets its name from the colour of this material. Windows were placed in locations important to the function of the rooms they illuminated, thus giving the exterior an irregular look and prioritizing the individual user of the home over an underlying and rigid formal order of the exterior.

STOTFOLD HOUSE, Bromley, London, England, 1907, Thomas Phillips Figgis, architect.

Giving rise to an unusual form and irregular mass, this Arts and Crafts home demonstrates the characteristic of the style without reliance on vernacular reference. The home is designed to connect to the landscape and in this case the garden. Extended patios on both primary facades along with very large areas of glass work together to accentuate this connection to nature.

FRANK LLOYD WRIGHT HOME AND STUDIO, Oak Park, Illinois, US, 1889, Frank Lloyd Wright, architect.

As an early precursor to Wright's own Prairie School style, the home rejects the Victorian fussiness prevalent during this time. The original building was designed as a modest Shingle style home with a large gabled facade. Wright added to and expanded the home over the years, experimenting with his ideas for domestic architecture.

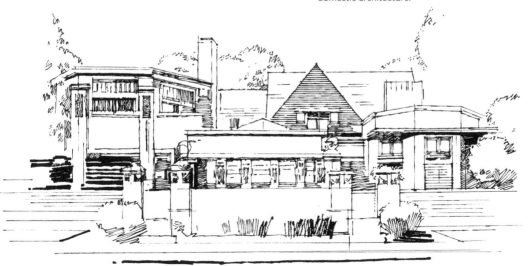

ROBERT R. BLACKER HOUSE, Pasadena, California, US, 1907, Greene and Greene, architects.

Everything in this house was custom designed down to the smallest detail, as was the practice of architects Greene and Greene. The exterior is made with old-growth redwood and Douglas fir with leaded-glass doors and windows. The house has a distinct horizontal emphasis, with broad overhangs and exposed rafters adding visual detail.

HORNIMAN MUSEUM, Forest Hill, London, England, 1898–1901, Charles Harrison Townsend, architect.

This purpose-designed museum is made of Doulting stone – a granular limestone – and features a large, ornate clock tower and a Greco-Roman mural embedded in the front, rounded gable. The house and tower have soft-edged, stone corners, effectively imbuing the architecture with an organic, natural aesthetic.

GODDARDS HOUSE, Dringhouses, York, England, 1927, Walter Brierley, architect.

The house has an offset symmetry that relates to the garden and reflects in the lily pond on the exterior. The structure is made of locally produced brick arranged in a variety of patterns on the gable fronts of the house.

STONEYWELL, Ulverscroft, England, 1898–99, Ernest Gimson, architect.

Designed as a summer residence, this home embraces the vernacular aesthetic important to the Arts and Crafts movement. The house is built from local stone and uses exposed bedrock as a natural foundation, further serving to connect the home to its rural surroundings.

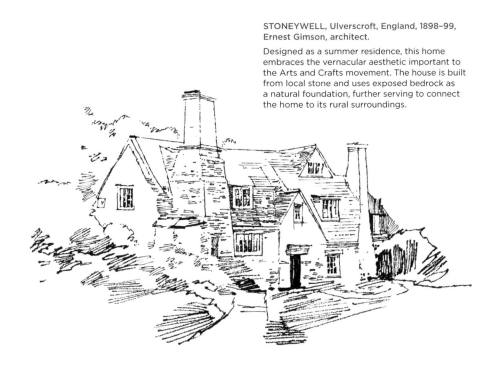

ART NOUVEAU
LATE NINETEENTH TO EARLY TWENTIETH CENTURIES

Established as an entirely new style devoid of historicism, Art Nouveau impacted the design world profoundly. Art, graphic design, fashion, jewellery, textiles, architecture, interior design and furniture: every element imaginable was influenced by the new visual language. Characterized by flowing forms and sinuous organic lines, often including plant motifs or female figurative elements, the style typically embraces asymmetric principles.

ART NOUVEAU KEY FEATURES:

- **asymmetry**
- **undulating lines**
- **whiplash curves**
- **organic ornament**
- **sinuous ornament**
- **flowing forms**

MAISON COILLIOT, Lille, France, 1898–1900, Hector Guimard, architect.

The facade of this house is asymmetrically balanced with intertwining materials of green enamelled volcanic rock, wrought iron and wood. The building actually has two facades: one that aligns with the neighbouring buildings and one that recedes at an angle away from the street. The arches on the ground floor vary in scale, with the smaller of the two forming the entrance to the apartments above the shopfront. The door is framed with a semicircular arch but is formed with an organic curve that matches the curve of the unique transom window directly above the door.

OLD ENGLAND BUILDING, BRUSSELS, Belgium, 1898–99, Paul Saintenoy, architect.

Once a department store, this building now houses the Museum of Musical Instruments. Built with a steel superstructure, the facade is marked with a protruding central oriel bay, supported on metal brackets. The crown of the building is a large, arched attic. The metalwork supporting the glass is extremely delicate, sinuous, and organic.

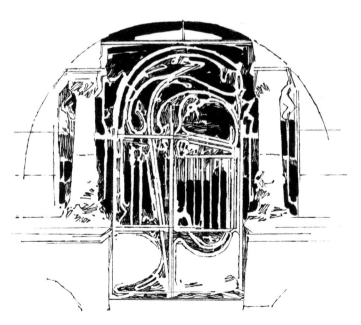

CASTEL BÉRANGER, Paris, France, 1895–98, Hector Guimard, architect.

This residential building holds thirty-six apartments, and its ornament was inspired largely by natural elements such as curving plants and flowers. This gateway is the primary entrance to the building and rests within a large, round stone arch flanked by organic columns with unusual Art Nouveau capitals and pedestals. The gate itself is a mix of sinuous lines and copper panels, its lightness a direct contrast to the weight of the stone facade.

HILL HOUSE, Helensburgh, Scotland, 1902–4, Charles Rennie Mackintosh and Margaret MacDonald, architects.

As Mackintosh's most significant domestic commission, the Hill House stands as a dignified mix of traditional Scottish architecture – with its staid, thick exterior – and the personal delicacy of the interiors. Constructed with Portland cement render, the exterior is balanced with an asymmetry that reflects the necessities of the interior, which is rich with elegant ornamentation in furniture, textiles, painted surfaces, lighting fixtures, carved wood, stained glass and other everyday objects. This home is in the Glasgow School style, a unique subset of Art Nouveau.

CASA BATLLÓ, Barcelona, Spain, 1904–6, Antoni Gaudí, architect.

The original building was constructed by a professor of Gaudí's, Emilio Sala Cortés, but a change of ownership gave Gaudí the opportunity to work on the project. The plan was to demolish the existing building, but Gaudí insisted that it remain and instead devised a clever plan to change the facade and rework the interior partitioning and the connection to the exterior through the addition of patios and balconettes. The facade is a breathtaking, undulating mosaic of broken ceramic tiles punctuated with ovoid openings and concluding with a rolling roof that some say resembles the back of a dragon.

HOTEL CENTRAL PRAGUE, Prague, Czech Republic, 1899–1902, Friedrich Ohmann, Alois Dryák and Bedrich Bendelmayer, architects.

One of the oldest Art Nouveau hotels in Prague, the facade has a central ornamental section that reaches up multiple levels. The entrance is covered with a glass and metal canopy, and just above that a filigreed tree motif supports and wraps around the elongated oriel bay that is capped with an eyebrow valance. Originally designed as a hotel and theatre, the main interior lobby, with its ornate ironwork, curved glass, and metal ceiling, opulent stained glass and arched barrel vault, describes a time when this building defined luxury.

TOPIČ BUILDING, Prague, Czech Republic, 1904, Osvald Polivka, architect.

With a facade designed by Polivka – the architect of the famous Municipal House in Prague, also in the Art Nouveau style – the Topič Building incorporates mosaics and relief sculptures in stucco depicting floral wreaths and swags. Polivka was one of the most important Art Nouveau architects of his time in Prague, designing many landmarks around the city.

PARIS MÉTRO ENTRANCES, Paris, France, 1900–13, Hector Guimard, architect.

Using cast iron and amber glass moulded to form incredible, stylized plant forms of natural delight, these designs served as the initial entrances to the Paris Métro system. Guimard's choice of material, in particular cast iron, was not only less expensive to produce in multiples but also required less space, an issue on some of the tighter sites. Eighty-six of these installations still exist today and are considered a national treasure – a designation that was not the case at their inception.

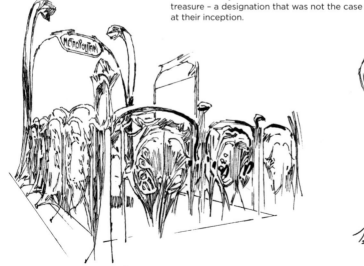

CAUCHIE HOUSE, Brussels, Belgium, 1905, Paul Cauchie, architect.

Cauchie, an architect and decorator, designed this house with his wife Lina Voet as a private residence for his family. They were inspired by the Glasgow School style of ornamentation, as seen in the detail around the window. The decoration focuses less on plant-like forms and more on a subtle interpretation of the female form.

MAISON ST-CYR, Brussels, Belgium, 1901–3, Gustave Strauven, architect.

At a mere 4 m (13 ft) wide, this extravagant house is incredibly tall and narrow. The facade is layered with glass and wrought iron to create a vertical explosion of Art Nouveau decor. Strauven was a student of Victor Horta, a master of the style.

4

MODERN AND CONTEMPORARY

ART DECO
TWENTIETH CENTURY

The Art Deco style is synonymous with luxury, yet is accessible to all, encompassing all arts, architecture, design, visual arts, as well as everyday objects. The name Art Deco is derived from the International Exhibition of Modern Decorative and Industrial Arts held in Paris in 1925 – the Arts Décoratifs. Intended to re-establish Paris as the centre of design, the exhibition brought together modern ideas on design, while referencing scale, proportion and symmetry from Classical Greek and Roman examples. The style was heavily influenced by the geometric references of Cubism, as well as a nod towards Eastern cultures such as Japan, China, Persia and India.

ART DECO KEY FEATURES:

- geometric patterns
- rectilinear lines
- curved building forms
- glamour and luxury
- reinterpretation of Classical elements
- low-relief sculptural ornamentation
- detailed craftsmanship

ODEON CINEMA, Kingstanding, England, 1935–36, Harry Weedon and Cecil Clavering, architects.

As the first cinema in the Odeon chain for Oscar Deutsch, this brick Art Deco theatre set the standard for others in the chain. With a large curved front and vertical billboard, it is a quintessential representation of Art Deco architectural drama.

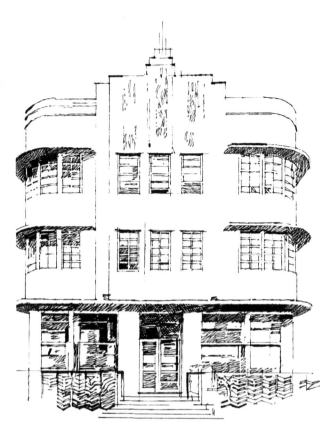

MARLIN HOTEL, Miami, Florida, US, 1939, L. Murray Dixon, architect.

As one of Miami's first boutique hotels, this South Beach landmark is three storeys tall, with a prominent ornamental vertical thrust over the entrance, and curved glass and sun shields wrapping around each side of the building.

MUTUAL BUILDING, Cape Town, South Africa, 1936–39, Louw & Louw Architects, architects.

These sculptures, located above one of the entrances, are carved in granite and represent the nine ethnic groups of Africa. The building, built in reinforced concrete and clad in granite, forms a ziggurat structure with vertical angled or triangled windows extending up and down the height of the building.

BOSTON AVENUE METHODIST CHURCH, Tulsa, Oklahoma, US, 1927–29, Adah Robinson and Bruce Goff, architects.

Below: The church, with its extraordinary vertical emphasis, appears to be reaching for the heavens. It is made of Indiana limestone and Minnesota granite, with terracotta sculptures by Denver sculptor Robert Garrison.

Above: Garrison's figural sculptures at the main entrance to the church.

NEW INDIA ASSURANCE BUILDING, Mumbai, India, 1936, Master, Sathe and Bhuta with N. G. Pansare, architects.

The elongated facade, made of reinforced concrete, is decorated with substantial vertical fins of sculpted figures, accentuating the monumental impression. The Indian Institute of Architects was instrumental in the application of Art Deco throughout Mumbai. Architects were attracted to the sleek, modern aesthetic and sought commissions that could showcase the style.

CHRYSLER BUILDING, New York City, New York, US, 1928–30, William Van Alen, architect.

As part of the great skyscraper race in the city in the 1920s, the building's spire was designed to extend into the clouds and glorify the machine age. The spire and crown are clad in stainless steel and constructed with seven radiating terraced arches inset with triangular windows. While difficult to see from the ground, the crown is a significant landmark in the Manhattan skyline.

BERKELEY SHORE HOTEL,
Miami, Florida, US, 1940, Albert
Anis, architect.

Located in the Art Deco Historic
District of Miami Beach, Florida,
this hotel is one of many
spectacular Art Deco structures
in the area, some of which were
part of a second phase of the
style after the crash of the stock
market in 1929. Slightly less
decorative with a less exuberant
formal language, the buildings
represent a shift in the style
due to the economic situation.

HOOVER BUILDING CAFETERIA, London,
England, 1933, Wallis, Gilbert & Partners,
architects.

Designed as a support building to feed
employees at the Hoover Building, the canteen is
a quintessential Art Deco structure. With curved
volumes of glass framing the entrance, the central
triangulated window extends upwards through the
face of the building, reaching towards its pinnacle.

THE DAILY TELEGRAPH BUILDING, Napier, New Zealand, 1932, E. A. Williams, architect.

The Art Deco style was selected for this building for practical reasons. The previous building had burned down and the earthquake of 1931 had the community concerned. Art Deco proved to be a modern-thinking, forward-looking style – and it was also stable. Constructed of reinforced concrete, the building was resistant to fire, and the low-relief sculpture reduced the risk of falling masonry during an earthquake.

CINE-TEATRO FAUSTO, Havana, Cuba, 1938, Santurnino Parajón, architect.

With strong vertical elements defining the entrance, and curved edges as the building turns the corner of the block, this Art Deco theatre achieves the nature of the style without the reliance on window form. Crenellations at the roof line, as well as at the elevated porch along the side, demonstrate the style's use of low-relief sculpture as decoration.

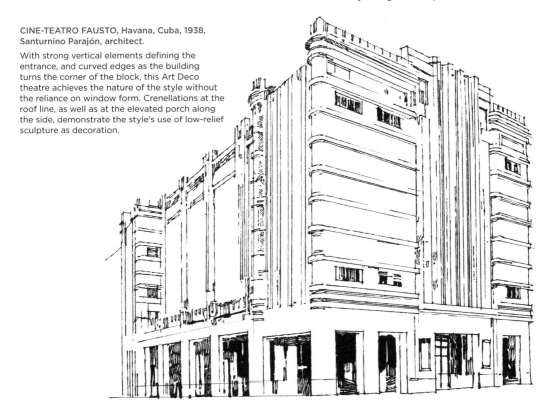

EXPRESSIONISM
TWENTIETH CENTURY

Expressionism was born from the desire, post-World War I, to design structures that evoked emotion. Tied in with the Expressionist arts movement occurring in Germany, designers sought forms that were biomorphic, anamorphic and, ultimately, expressive. Outside of Germany, the Amsterdam School style of architecture played a significant role in the movement. The brick housing developments in Amsterdam experimented in Expressionism through complex, amorphous yet monolithic structures, integrating multiple expressive forms into one large block.

EXPRESSIONISM KEY FEATURES:

- **dramatic gestures of form**
- **anthropomorphic**
- **expressive form**
- **monolithic material choices**
- **building as sculpture**
- **free-flowing organic forms**

HET SCHIP, Amsterdam, the Netherlands, 1917–21, Michel de Klerk, architect.

Left: The energetic forming of brickwork in this urban housing project paved the way for the Amsterdam School of architecture. This three-block complex provided enough area for the architect to experiment with practical construction solutions – brick – in conjunction with rhythmic architectural forms. The exterior can be considered as a singular sculptural assembly and encompasses over one hundred housing units, a community hall and a post office.

Above: This detail of an eyebrow window rises from the surface of the facade to create a triangulated effect, providing light and views from multiple directions.

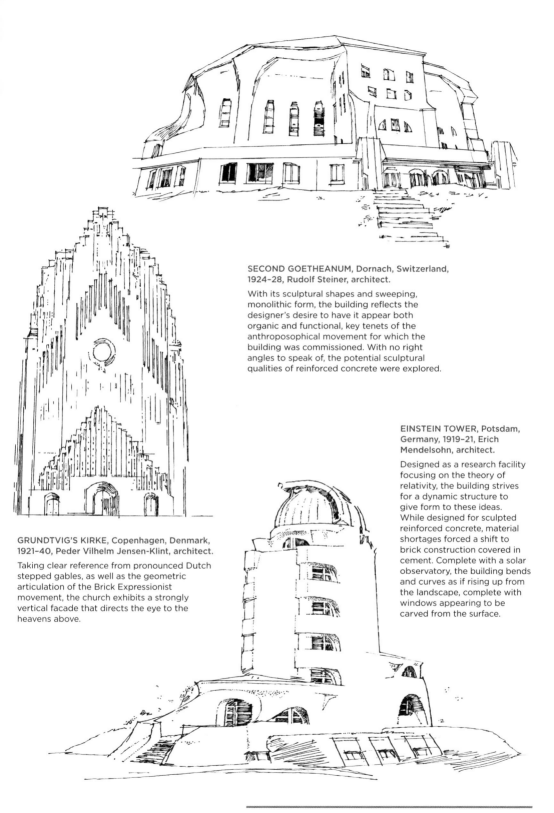

SECOND GOETHEANUM, Dornach, Switzerland, 1924–28, Rudolf Steiner, architect.

With its sculptural shapes and sweeping, monolithic form, the building reflects the designer's desire to have it appear both organic and functional, key tenets of the anthroposophical movement for which the building was commissioned. With no right angles to speak of, the potential sculptural qualities of reinforced concrete were explored.

EINSTEIN TOWER, Potsdam, Germany, 1919–21, Erich Mendelsohn, architect.

Designed as a research facility focusing on the theory of relativity, the building strives for a dynamic structure to give form to these ideas. While designed for sculpted reinforced concrete, material shortages forced a shift to brick construction covered in cement. Complete with a solar observatory, the building bends and curves as if rising up from the landscape, complete with windows appearing to be carved from the surface.

GRUNDTVIG'S KIRKE, Copenhagen, Denmark, 1921–40, Peder Vilhelm Jensen-Klint, architect.

Taking clear reference from pronounced Dutch stepped gables, as well as the geometric articulation of the Brick Expressionist movement, the church exhibits a strongly vertical facade that directs the eye to the heavens above.

MODERNISM
TWENTIETH CENTURY

With a focus on simplicity, minimalism and a rejection of ornament, Modernism allowed designers to concentrate on the functionality of buildings. New materials and construction technologies led to innovative open-plan interiors, as well as taller and lighter buildings. Walter Gropius, founder of the Bauhaus, and Charles-Édouard Jeanneret, known as Le Corbusier, were two of the pioneering architects of Modernism. With his highly influential text *Towards a New Architecture*, Le Corbusier implored architects to reject traditional forms and embrace modernist ideals. Summarized, his five points are as follows: to replace walls with a grid of load-bearing columns, pilotis; to emphasize the open floor plan generated without reliance on load-bearing walls; to separate the facade from structural components; to use long, horizontal window apertures to light rooms equally; and to utilize roof gardens.

MODERNISM KEY FEATURES:

- simple geometries
- emphasis on function
- little or no ornament
- smooth surfaces
- minimal material palette
- glass, steel and concrete
- open-plan interiors

BAUHAUS BUILDING, Dessau, Germany, 1925–26, Walter Gropius, architect.

Designed to support the school's core values of a unified vision and holistic approach to the creative fields, the building represents the emerging relationship between industrial mechanization and the arts. Built with reinforced concrete, brick and glass, the structure is organized in a pinwheel form with bridges connecting the three sections. Large glass curtain walls wrap the corners and provide ample light, as well as views into the school from the exterior.

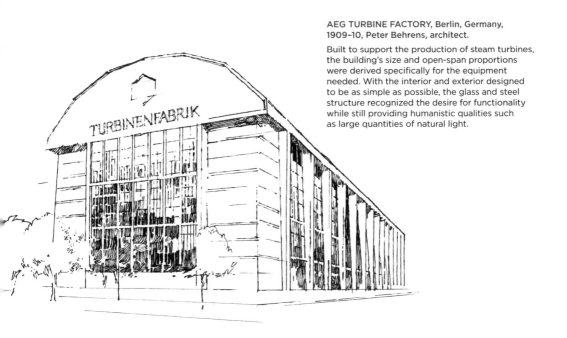

AEG TURBINE FACTORY, Berlin, Germany, 1909–10, Peter Behrens, architect.

Built to support the production of steam turbines, the building's size and open-span proportions were derived specifically for the equipment needed. With the interior and exterior designed to be as simple as possible, the glass and steel structure recognized the desire for functionality while still providing humanistic qualities such as large quantities of natural light.

EAMES HOUSE, Pacific Palisades, California, US, 1949, Charles and Ray Eames, architects.

Designed as a home and studio for this husband and wife team, the house – also known as Case Study House No. 8 – was created as part of the Case Study House Program in conjuction with *Arts & Architecture* magazine. For this particular home, the focus was on using prefabricated materials to create an open living environment.

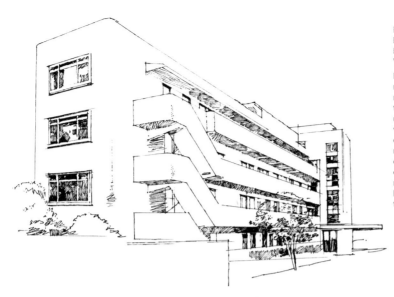

ISOKON BUILDING (The Lawn Road Flats), Hampstead, London, England, 1932–34, Wells Coates, architect.

Designed as a forward-thinking modernist experiment in minimalist communal living, this apartment building's units have tiny kitchens with a connection to a communal kitchen. The reinforced concrete form emphasizes the connective circulation elements through repetitive stairs and strong horizontal banding for the pathways.

UNESCO HEADQUARTERS, Paris, France, 1952–58, Marcel Breuer, Pier Luigi Nervi and Bernard Zehrfuss, architects.

The main building in this complex is seven storeys tall, raised on large tapered pilotis, and is in the shape of an elongated three-pointed star. In collaboration with Marcel Breuer, significant design contributions were made by Beverly Loraine Greene, the first African American female architect registered in the United States.

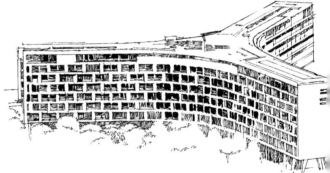

BARCELONA PAVILION, Barcelona, Spain, 1928–29, Ludwig Mies van der Rohe, architect.

Designed with thin planes of materials, the structure emphasizes the horizontal plane through the pronounced overhangs of the flat roof. Once inside, offset vertical planes encourage meandering while simultaneously orienting framed views to other portions of the pavilion and the site beyond.

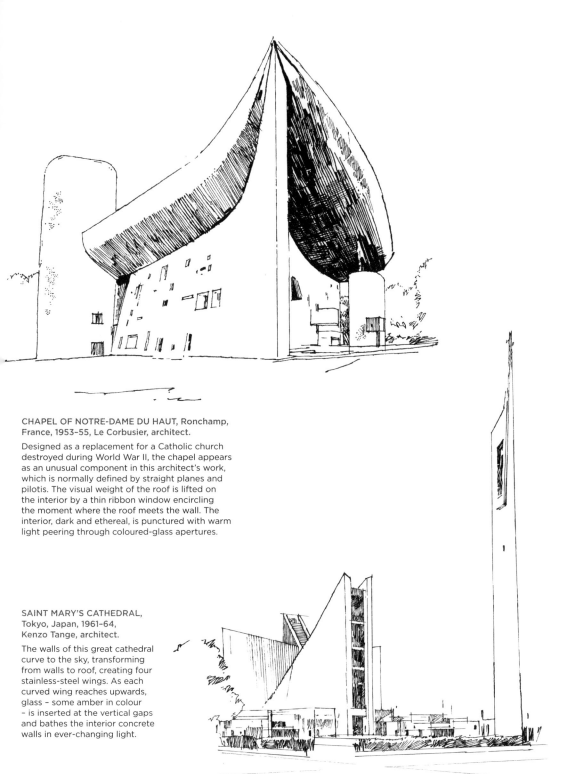

CHAPEL OF NOTRE-DAME DU HAUT, Ronchamp, France, 1953–55, Le Corbusier, architect.

Designed as a replacement for a Catholic church destroyed during World War II, the chapel appears as an unusual component in this architect's work, which is normally defined by straight planes and pilotis. The visual weight of the roof is lifted on the interior by a thin ribbon window encircling the moment where the roof meets the wall. The interior, dark and ethereal, is punctured with warm light peering through coloured-glass apertures.

SAINT MARY'S CATHEDRAL, Tokyo, Japan, 1961–64, Kenzo Tange, architect.

The walls of this great cathedral curve to the sky, transforming from walls to roof, creating four stainless-steel wings. As each curved wing reaches upwards, glass – some amber in colour – is inserted at the vertical gaps and bathes the interior concrete walls in ever-changing light.

SOLOMON R. GUGGENHEIM MUSEUM, New York City, New York, US, 1953–59, Frank Lloyd Wright, architect.

The curved, spiralling exterior form of this iconic New York building directly reflects the continuous floor plane on the interior, beginning at ground level and moving up through the six-storey height of the building on an inclined plane. The horizontal bands surround an open central atrium and reach out to expanded galleries at each level.

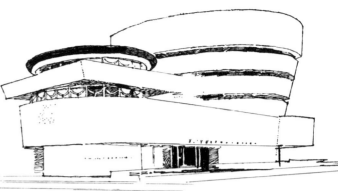

LA CONCHA MOTEL, Las Vegas, Nevada, US, 1961, Paul R. Williams, architect.

The sweeping futuristic appearance of the motel lobby put this building squarely in the category of Googie architecture – an American subgenre of Mid-Century Modernism characterized by Atomic and Space Age symbols and forms. The motel lobby was saved from demolition and moved to a new location in 2007 to serve as the Neon Museum's visitor centre.

UNITED STATES AIR FORCE ACADEMY CADET CHAPEL, Colorado Springs, Colorado, US, 1959–62, Skidmore, Owings & Merrill, architects.

This striking chapel is formed directly from its structural system of seventeen rows of spires reaching into the sky. The spires are formed with tubular steel frames made up of one hundred identical tetrahedrons. Each tetrahedron is wrapped in aluminium panels and spaced a foot apart, with coloured glass filling the gaps between each one.

FALLINGWATER, Mill Run, Pennsylvania, US, 1936–37, Frank Lloyd Wright, architect.

Designed to synthesize building, living and nature, the house is perched alongside a stream with cantilevered exterior terrace planes extending and hovering above the wet ground plane below. With extensive use of glass virtually eliminating normative conditions such as corners, the interior of the house visually extends into the natural site.

VILLA DIRICKZ, Brussels, Belgium, 1929–33, Marcel Leborgne, architect.

Largely constructed of concrete and steel, this home forms two primary volumes – a four-storey shifting cube and a four-storey cylindrical exterior stair. The cubic form is broken down with large horizontal bands defining the exterior spaces that appear to slide back and forth along windowed edges, creating the illusion of displacement.

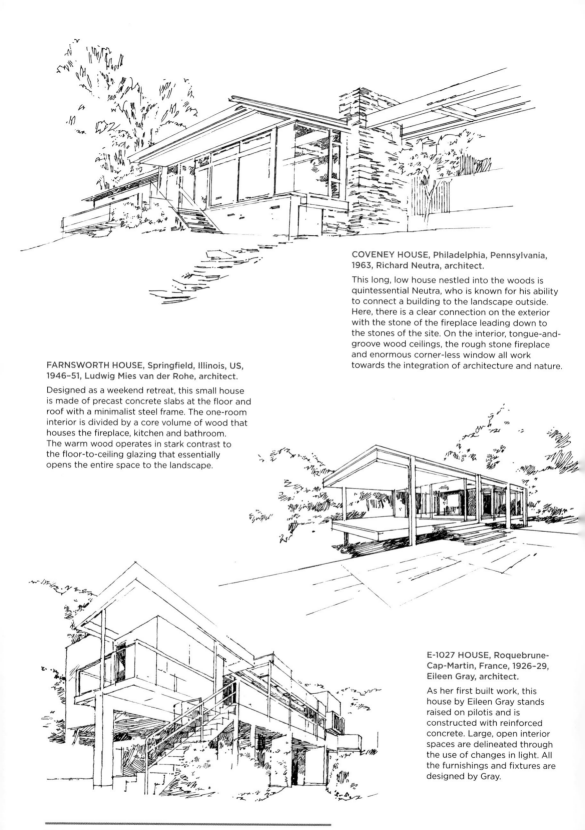

COVENEY HOUSE, Philadelphia, Pennsylvania, 1963, Richard Neutra, architect.

This long, low house nestled into the woods is quintessential Neutra, who is known for his ability to connect a building to the landscape outside. Here, there is a clear connection on the exterior with the stone of the fireplace leading down to the stones of the site. On the interior, tongue-and-groove wood ceilings, the rough stone fireplace and enormous corner-less window all work towards the integration of architecture and nature.

FARNSWORTH HOUSE, Springfield, Illinois, US, 1946–51, Ludwig Mies van der Rohe, architect.

Designed as a weekend retreat, this small house is made of precast concrete slabs at the floor and roof with a minimalist steel frame. The one-room interior is divided by a core volume of wood that houses the fireplace, kitchen and bathroom. The warm wood operates in stark contrast to the floor-to-ceiling glazing that essentially opens the entire space to the landscape.

E-1027 HOUSE, Roquebrune-Cap-Martin, France, 1926–29, Eileen Gray, architect.

As her first built work, this house by Eileen Gray stands raised on pilotis and is constructed with reinforced concrete. Large, open interior spaces are delineated through the use of changes in light. All the furnishings and fixtures are designed by Gray.

PHILLIPS EXETER ACADEMY LIBRARY, Exeter, New Hampshire, US, 1965–72, Louis I. Kahn, architect.

The interior of this library makes clear its spatial organization: a square in plan with a multistorey square atrium rising above the circulation desk in the centre. The use of circle and square on the interior not only opens the visual corridors between floors, it also references the relationship between the geometries and the human form, as described by Leonardo da Vinci in his Vitruvian Man drawing, which was a recurring theme for Khan.

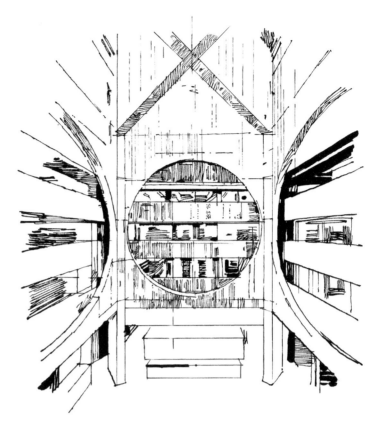

PALÁCIO DA ALVORADA, Brasilia, Brazil, 1957–58, Oscar Niemeyer, architect.

Designed as a presidential palace for the new city of Brasilia, now the capital of Brazil, the structure is one of several by Niemeyer in the city. With a distinctive colonnade of swooping structural elements holding up a long, flat horizontal plane for the roof, the low structure establishes a delicate balance and graceful partnership between strong horizontal and vertical elements.

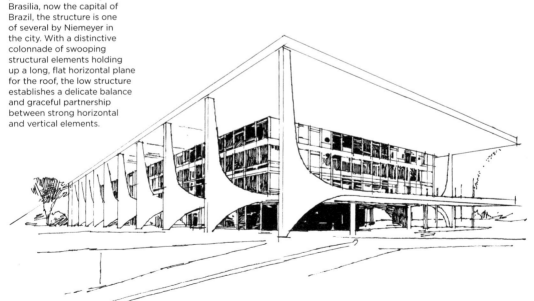

CONSTRUCTIVISM
EARLY TWENTIETH CENTURY

Constructivism was a radical, short-lived architectural style that began in Russia in the early twentieth century. Focused on reflecting and adapting to societal progress, the style rejected traditional forms of architecture in search of new geometries supported by specific engineering solutions. In this way, the work attempted to merge science, art and everyday life to promote the ideals of society after the Russian Revolution.

CONSTRUCTIVISM KEY FEATURES:

- **non-referential**
- **massive forms**
- **substantial engineering solutions**
- **specific to Russia**

NARKOMFIN BUILDING,
Moscow, Russia, 1928–30,
Moisei Ginzburg and Ignaty
Milinis, architects.

This long apartment block is made of reinforced concrete elevated on pilotis. With communal kitchens and laundry facilities, as well as social programmes such as the library and gymnasium, the building was designed to facilitate a new social order by creating intersections of everyday life.

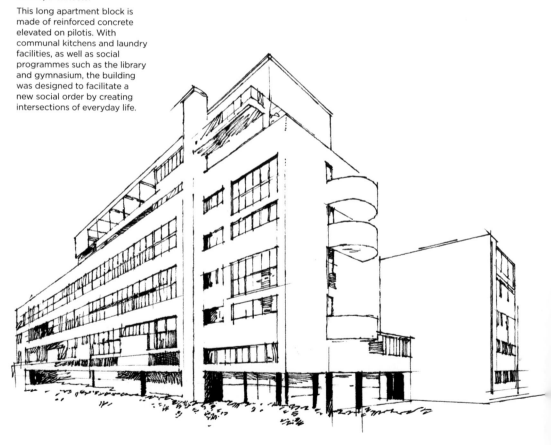

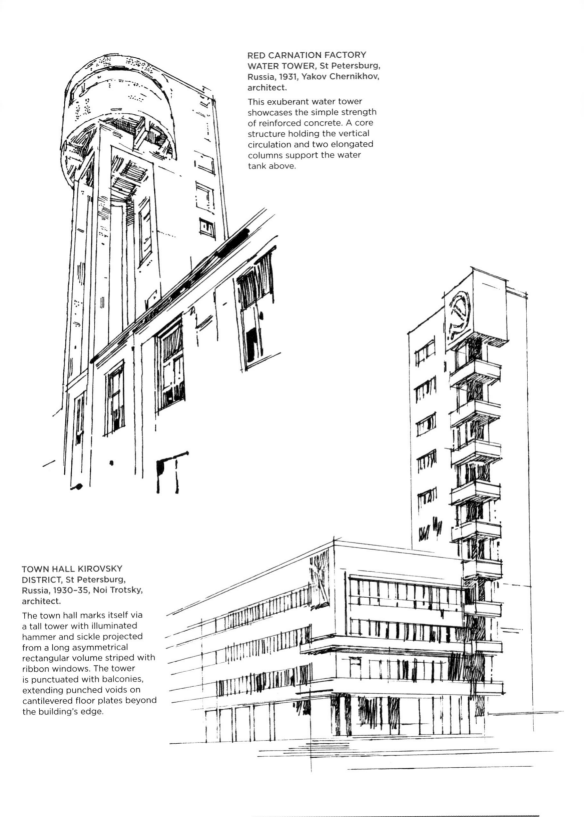

RED CARNATION FACTORY WATER TOWER, St Petersburg, Russia, 1931, Yakov Chernikhov, architect.

This exuberant water tower showcases the simple strength of reinforced concrete. A core structure holding the vertical circulation and two elongated columns support the water tank above.

TOWN HALL KIROVSKY DISTRICT, St Petersburg, Russia, 1930–35, Noi Trotsky, architect.

The town hall marks itself via a tall tower with illuminated hammer and sickle projected from a long asymmetrical rectangular volume striped with ribbon windows. The tower is punctuated with balconies, extending punched voids on cantilevered floor plates beyond the building's edge.

KAUCHUK FACTORY CLUB, Moscow, Russia, 1927–29, Konstantin Melnikov, architect.

Developed as part of a new building typology, the workers' club, this particular club is in the shape of a quarter of a cylinder and reaches out to the street with a massive bifurcated curvilinear staircase. Intended to host not just the elite but also the masses of working society, the clubs provided a retreat from factory conditions and helped frame a new social order.

KRASNY PROSPEKT 11, Novosibirsk, Russia, 1931–34, B. A. Gordeyev, D. A. Ageyev and B. A. Bitkin, architects.

This is one of six residential buildings, along with a school, in the Kuzbassugol Building Complex, which was designed to encompass social needs. The complex reflects the intersection of two rectilinear volumes, one horizontal and one vertical, culminating with a clock tower at the urban corner.

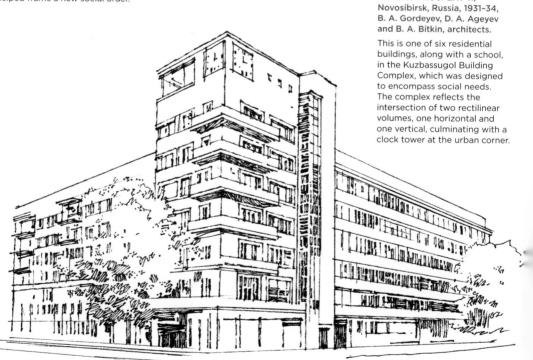

MELNIKOV HOUSE, Moscow, Russia, 1927–29, Konstantin Melnikov, architect.

Consisting of two overlapping cylindrical towers adorned with hexagonal windows, the Melnikov House stands as a representation of constructivist structural experimentation. The honeycomb brick grid and geometric windows were developed as a way to minimize material use, to make the structure more affordable.

BRUTALISM
TWENTIETH CENTURY

Brutalism, from *béton-brut* – French for raw concrete – emerged in the mid-twentieth century as a response to the overly smooth and perfected finishes of Modernist architecture. Typical materials include brick and poured-in-place concrete, whose surfaces often show the pattern of wooden planks used as forms during construction. It is characterized by massive, monolithic forms with a strong underpinning of geometric form, often expressing, through repetitive elements, the individuality of users within the mass of the whole.

BRUTALISM KEY FEATURES:

- **poured-in-place concrete**
- **raw concrete**
- **monolithic forms**
- **pilotis (load-bearing columns)**
- **repetitive elements, particularly apertures**

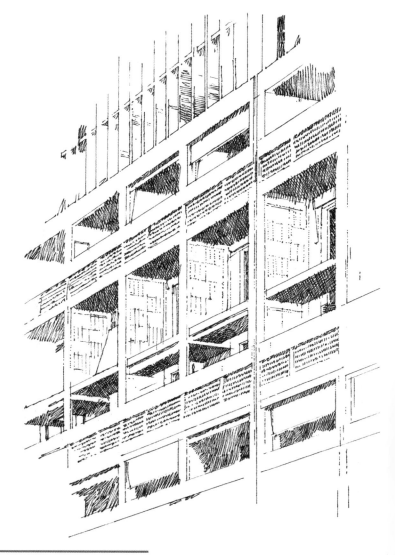

UNITÉ D'HABITATION, Marseille, France, 1947–52, Le Corbusier, architect.

Three hundred and thirty-seven two-level apartments configured over twelve storeys are innovatively interlocked such that an interior corridor is needed only on every third floor. Each apartment has deep-set windows and balconies. The entire structure sits on pilotis and boasts two shopping streets, a hotel and a rooftop terrace. The surfaces are marked by poured-in-place concrete board forms.

SAINTE MARIE DE LA TOURETTE, near Lyon, France, 1956–60, Le Corbusier, architect.

This monastery building is raised on pilotis that touch the ground lightly, amplifying the mass of the structure above. One hundred monastic cells are lit by horizontal strip windows on the interior courtyard facade and deep balconies on the exterior facade, to mitigate both natural light and shade. Public areas have floor-to-ceiling glass, with grass rooftops to offset the building's footprint.

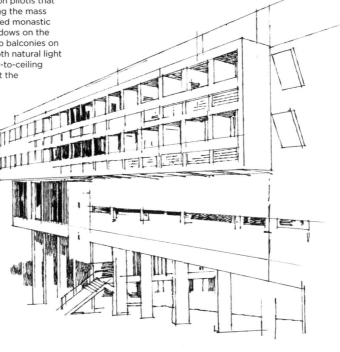

MINISTRY OF HIGHWAY CONSTRUCTION (now Bank of Georgia), Tbilisi, Georgia, 1975, George Chakhava and Zurab Jalaghania, architects.

The monumental interlocking concrete grid consists of five horizontal bars of offices and three vertical circulation cores with stair and lift systems. Large segments of the structure are lifted off the ground to minimize the impact to nature.

SHRI RAM CENTRE FOR ART AND CULTURE, New Delhi, India, 1966–69, Shiv Nath Prasad, architect.

Massive form defines primary function in this building. The cylindrical volume is the main auditorium, and hovering above is a large rectangular multi-functional space that cantilevers above columns, exposing the structural underbelly of concrete: a two-way joist slab, also known as a waffle slab. Above, a brise-soleil – popularized by Le Corbusier – is implemented through tall vertical concrete fins used to manage sun exposure to the interior of the building.

NEW DELHI MUNICIPAL COUNCIL BUILDING, New Delhi, India, 1983, Kuldip Singh, architect.

The form of this building is intended to be seen as a mighty, forceful mass emerging from the ground, and rising up to express the more sculptural quality of concrete.

WELBECK STREET CAR PARK, City of Westminster, London, England, 1971, Michael Blampied & Partners, architects.

Relished by architects for its impressive diamond-grid surface of pre-cast concrete modules, the facade characterized the mundane parking garage as a gem within the city block. This building was controversially demolished in 2019, amid demands for its preservation.

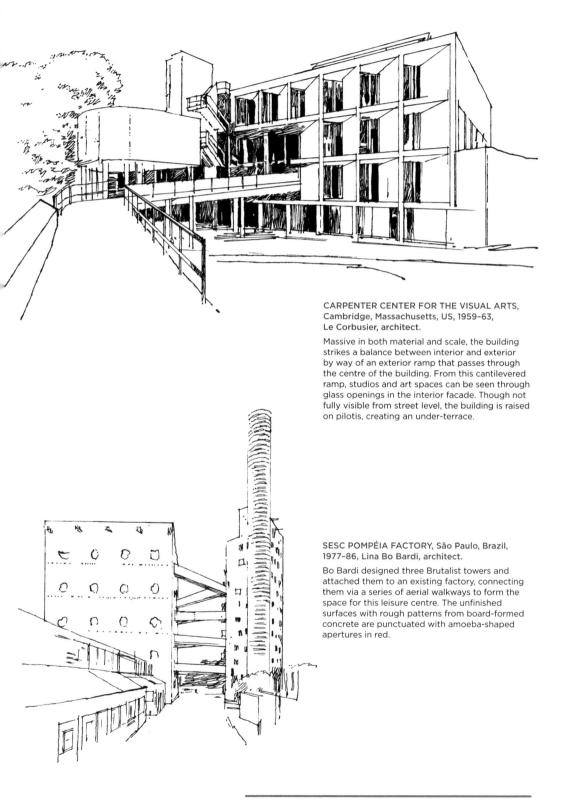

CARPENTER CENTER FOR THE VISUAL ARTS,
Cambridge, Massachusetts, US, 1959–63,
Le Corbusier, architect.

Massive in both material and scale, the building
strikes a balance between interior and exterior
by way of an exterior ramp that passes through
the centre of the building. From this cantilevered
ramp, studios and art spaces can be seen through
glass openings in the interior facade. Though not
fully visible from street level, the building is raised
on pilotis, creating an under-terrace.

SESC POMPÉIA FACTORY, São Paulo, Brazil,
1977–86, Lina Bo Bardi, architect.

Bo Bardi designed three Brutalist towers and
attached them to an existing factory, connecting
them via a series of aerial walkways to form the
space for this leisure centre. The unfinished
surfaces with rough patterns from board-formed
concrete are punctuated with amoeba-shaped
apertures in red.

METABOLISM
TWENTIETH CENTURY

During the rebuilding of Japan following World War II, Metabolism emerged as an attempt to think about architectural solutions on multiple scales, from a single structure to urban design. Primarily, Metabolists argued that architecture should be akin to a biological cell, adaptable, dynamic and able to transform – similar to the metabolic transformation of a living cell. These ideals were merged with traditional principles of Japanese culture, and even notions of monumentality, all focused on the rebuilding of society.

METABOLISM KEY FEATURES:

- specific to Japan
- modularity
- monumentality
- Japanese traditional values
- buildings were adaptable and designed for future change

YOYOGI NATIONAL GYMNASIUM, Tokyo, Japan, 1961–64, Kenzo Tange, architect.

Designed as a venue for swimming events for the 1964 Summer Olympics, the design of this gymnasium strives to address modern needs while simultaneously paying homage to traditional Japanese temple architecture – particularly through the two vertical elements at either end of the roof structure, as well as the sweeping form of the whole. Using a central structural spine, the suspended roof spins away in sweeping curves and blends with the curved form of the concrete base.

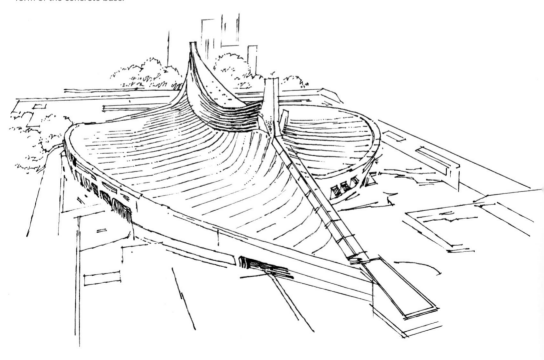

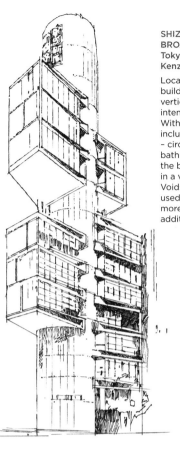

SHIZUOKA PRESS AND BROADCASTING CENTRE,
Tokyo, Japan, 1967,
Kenzo Tange, architect.

Located on a small site, the building is designed as a vertical megastructure and is intended to develop organically. With a central core that includes all necessary systems – circulation, structure, bathrooms, entrance lobbies – the building's capsules plug in in a variety of configurations. Voids between capsules are used as exterior terraces until more space is needed and an additional capsule is plugged in.

NAKAGIN CAPSULE TOWER, Tokyo, Japan, 1972,
Kisho Kurokawa, architect.

This two-towered building houses 140 self-contained, prefabricated capsules. Each capsule measures 2.4 x 4 m (8 x 13 ft), has one round window and is connected to the building at a concrete core. The capsules can be combined and connected to make larger living areas. The design intention of the building was to create a flexible system of living where anyone could 'plug in'.

HIROSHIMA PEACE MEMORIAL MUSEUM,
Hiroshima, Japan, 1949–55, Kenzo Tange, architect.

As a multi-part urban intervention leading from the Atomic Dome, the last remaining structure and considered to be located at the centre of the atomic bomb explosion, the museum building stands in rectilinear opposition to the mangled, melting structure of the dome. The urban scheme was intended to connect the past and the future with a public plaza dedicated to the people of Hiroshima. Tange combined the architectural principles of Corbusier with traditional Japanese elements of design, as evident in the brise-soleil elements of the building.

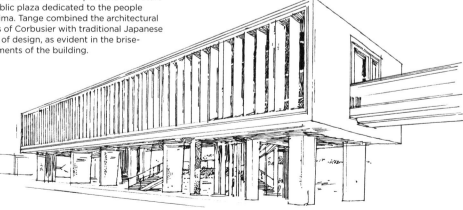

HIGH-TECH
TWENTIETH CENTURY

High-Tech architecture attempts to fully communicate how a building functions structurally, mechanically and systematically. It is seen as an honest and transparent expression, or even a celebration, of how things work. Typically, this style results in an architecture that has an industrial aesthetic, often with exposed services, circulation and structure. A by-product of the externalization of systems is the resultant openness of the interior, frequently manifested in large, wide-span, flexible spaces.

HIGH-TECH KEY FEATURES:

- exposed structures
- exposed mechanical systems
- steel, glass, concrete
- industrial aesthetic
- wide structural spans

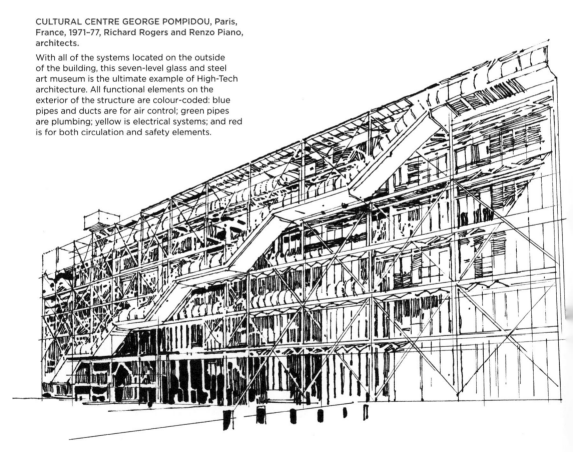

CULTURAL CENTRE GEORGE POMPIDOU, Paris, France, 1971–77, Richard Rogers and Renzo Piano, architects.

With all of the systems located on the outside of the building, this seven-level glass and steel art museum is the ultimate example of High-Tech architecture. All functional elements on the exterior of the structure are colour-coded: blue pipes and ducts are for air control; green pipes are plumbing; yellow is electrical systems; and red is for both circulation and safety elements.

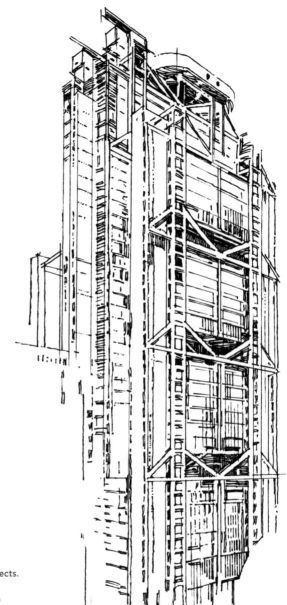

HSBC MAIN BUILDING,
Hong Kong, 1983–85,
Foster + Partners, architects.

This forty-seven-storey
building was designed in
modules: five steel modules,
prefabricated and shipped
onto site for construction.
The structure for the building
resides on the exterior,
effectively opening the centre
of the building for systems
of open space and circulation.

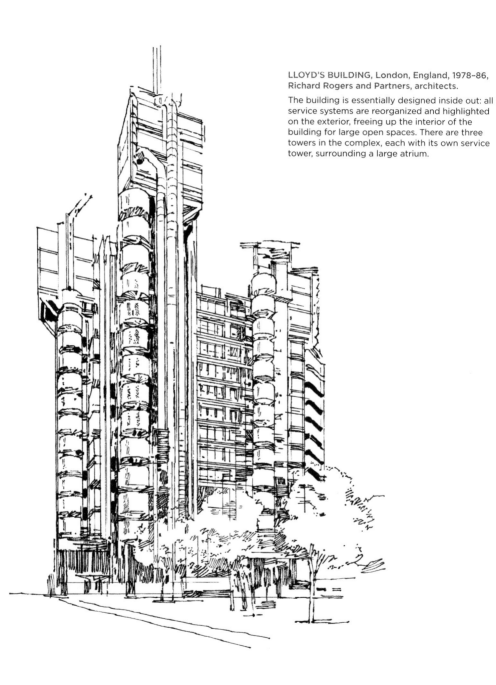

LLOYD'S BUILDING, London, England, 1978–86, Richard Rogers and Partners, architects.

The building is essentially designed inside out: all service systems are reorganized and highlighted on the exterior, freeing up the interior of the building for large open spaces. There are three towers in the complex, each with its own service tower, surrounding a large atrium.

SAINSBURY CENTRE FOR VISUAL ARTS,
Norwich, England, 1974–78, Foster + Partners,
architects.

With an exposed, prefabricated truss structure,
this simple building, clad in steel, clearly expresses
its open-space organization. The facade is
assembled entirely of glass, and the museum relies
on an open floor plan to disperse natural light to
spaces and galleries within the structure.

**INTERNATIONALES CONGRESS CENTRUM
BERLIN,** Berlin, Germany, 1975–79, Ralf Schüler
and Ursulina Schüler-Witte, architects.

Clad in metal and futuristic in appearance, this
is one of the largest High-Tech buildings, which
operated for decades as an international
conference centre. With an exposed structure
and round, protruding multi-level stairs, it sits
as a massive machine in the landscape.

POSTMODERNISM
TWENTIETH CENTURY

As a targeted move away from the aesthetic limits of Modernism, Postmodernism emerged as an antidote to the ills of the form-follows-function mantra. Led by Denise Scott Brown and Robert Venturi in their influential book *Learning from Las Vegas*, written with Steven Izemour, the movement recognizes a philosophical shift towards a more contextualized, symbolic and referential architecture. Postmodernist architecture attempts to create a new language of architecture, and while it references elements of Classical architecture, these are adapted for modern form. Colour, surface decoration, playful translation of building elements and even architectural irony define a movement that Venturi framed by saying, 'Less is a bore!'

POSTMODERNISM KEY FEATURES:

- playful character
- use of colour
- adaption of classic ideals to modern form
- architectural irony
- fragmented elements

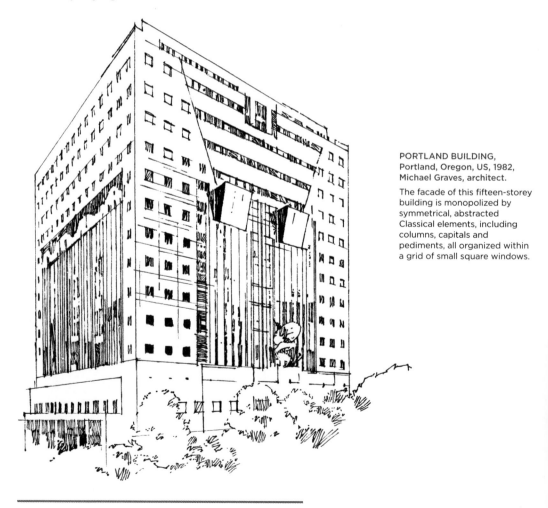

PORTLAND BUILDING, Portland, Oregon, US, 1982, Michael Graves, architect.

The facade of this fifteen-storey building is monopolized by symmetrical, abstracted Classical elements, including columns, capitals and pediments, all organized within a grid of small square windows.

VANCOUVER PUBLIC LIBRARY, Vancouver,
British Columbia, Canada, 1993–95, Safdie
Architects and Downs Archambault & Partners,
architects.

Books and services are housed in a nine-storey
cylinder wrapped in a spiralling wall structure that
acts as the facade. The interstitial space between
the cylinder and the curved colonnaded structure
creates an urban plaza that extends both inside
and outside.

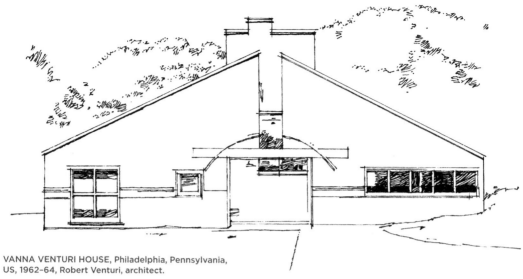

VANNA VENTURI HOUSE, Philadelphia, Pennsylvania, US, 1962–64, Robert Venturi, architect.

Considered to be one of the first pieces of Postmodernist architecture, this house for Venturi's mother retained some typical elements of Modernism, namely the horizontal ribbon window. However, the architect added ornamentation, an idea routinely refuted by Modernist architects. The front elevation is iconic as a representation of Postmodernism; the vertical opening at the pediment marking the entrance is in itself purely ornamental – there is no pediment at the back.

M2 BUILDING, Tokyo, Japan, 1989–91, Kengo Kuma, architect.

An early example of Kuma's work, and in stark contrast to his more recent elegant and sustainable projects, the M2 building is an expressive and experimental foray into Postmodern architecture. Constructed entirely of concrete, the building combines out-of-scale and out-of-place representations of Classical architecture.

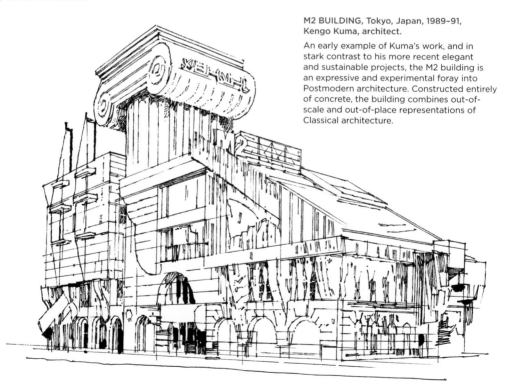

SAN CATALDO CEMETERY, Modena, Italy, 1971, Aldo Rossi, architect.

This red cube has geometric precision as its underpinning and stands as a memorial ossuary, intended to house the bones of the dead. It sits in solitude in a courtyard surrounded by other funerary buildings of contrasting grey and blue. The interior of the cube is a scaffold with multi-level access to individual niches designed for remains.

OFFICE BUILDING, Lugano, Switzerland, 1981–85, Mario Botta, architect.

Cubic in form, a solid corner treatment anchors the presence of the building within the urban block. The building stands as a monument of regularized red brick construction. The inner facade of steel and glass is revealed by the systematic removal of geometric portions of the brickwork.

DECONSTRUCTIVISM
TWENTIETH CENTURY ONWARDS

Deconstructivism was a direct reaction to Postmodernism and sought to dismantle understood assemblages of architecture. Focused on using a theoretical, linguistic approach to convey meaning, Deconstructivism relied on the understanding and then the referential discord of architectural elements. The style is ultimately an experiment in the systematic separation, dislocation, rearrangement and distortion of form. While the style does not follow rules, it does allow for the playful investigation of form and volume. The name is derived from the idea of 'deconstruction' advanced by philosopher Jacques Derrida and extends this semiotic inquiry of the relationship between text and meaning to architecture.

DECONSTRUCTIVISM KEY FEATURES:

- abstract forms
- deconstructed elements
- absence of symmetry
- absence of spatial harmony
- disassembled aesthetic

GUGGENHEIM MUSEUM BILBAO, Bilbao, Spain, 1993–97, Frank Gehry, architect.

Designed with a Deconstructivist approach, the building eschews straight edges and corners in favour of sweeping intersecting volumes. Silver titanium and Spanish limestone merge on the exterior to form a structure with no clear, definable edge. The shape shifts depending on position and view, in many ways similar to the experience of the interior.

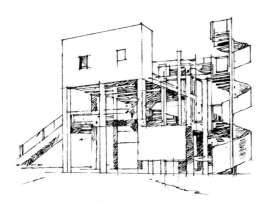

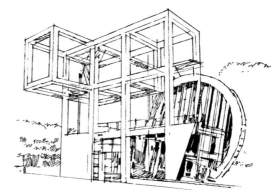

PARC DE LA VILLETTE, Paris, France, 1984–87,
Bernard Tschumi and Colin Fournier, architects.

With twenty-six follies scattered across this large
urban park, the intention of the architects was
to create a space that encourages activity and
connection. The follies – buildings designed
primarily as decoration but often referencing
something else entirely – are arranged in a large
grid and act as way-finding and orienting devices
for the park.

JEWISH MUSEUM BERLIN,
Berlin, Germany, 1992–2001,
Daniel Libeskind, architect.

A challenging commission
of epic meaning, the Jewish
Museum in Berlin can have
multiple visual interpretations.
However, one thing remains
steady: its uncanny ability
to simultaneously root and
disorient the visitor within
its sombre, cavernous spaces.
The slashes through the exterior
titanium-zinc facade give no
indication of floor levels or
organization within.

WEXNER CENTER FOR THE ARTS, Columbus, Ohio, US, 1987–89, Peter Eisenman and Richard Trott, architects.

As Eisenman's first Deconstructivist piece of architecture, the Wexner Center boasts many of the elemental tropes of the style, including the fragmenting of forms and the extreme layering of framed elements. While the building stands as if ignoring its context, the multiple allusions to iconic buildings in the area as well as systems of the city create a complex system of referential architecture.

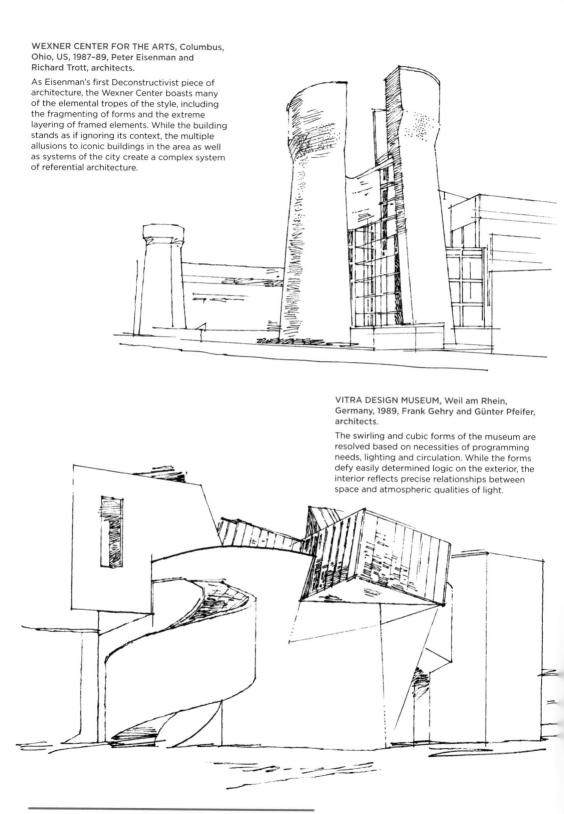

VITRA DESIGN MUSEUM, Weil am Rhein, Germany, 1989, Frank Gehry and Günter Pfeifer, architects.

The swirling and cubic forms of the museum are resolved based on necessities of programming needs, lighting and circulation. While the forms defy easily determined logic on the exterior, the interior reflects precise relationships between space and atmospheric qualities of light.

VITRA FIRE STATION, Weil am Rhein, Germany, 1989–93, Zaha Hadid, architect.

As Hadid's first built project, this fire house, now museum, is spatially formed with concrete planes bending, breaking and tilting in response to the surrounding landscape. A series of linear and layered walls separate and contain programmatic spaces, expressing the idea that the building could leap into action at any given moment.

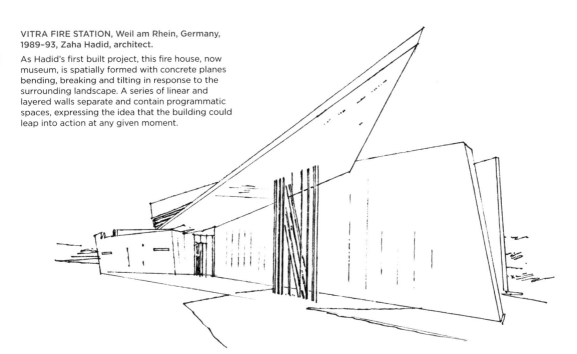

UFA CINEMA CENTRE, Dresden, Germany, 1993–98, Coop Himmelb(l)au, architects.

It is important to note that Deconstructivism isn't just about form; it can also relate to the function or perceived purpose of a building. Here, the architects strove to challenge the idea of the public building by deconstructing, redefining and reassembling notions of public space.

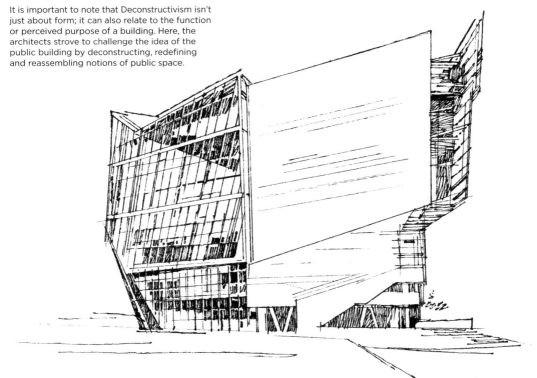

ECO-ARCHITECTURE
TWENTIETH CENTURY ONWARDS

A movement more than a style, Eco-Architecture maintains as its focus a moral imperative to design buildings that will have minimal impact on the environment during their construction process and while in use. Through their design, these buildings hold sustainability as their core value and implement efficient systems of energy use and production, promoting the responsible stewardship architecture can take in support of our environment.

ECO-ARCHITECTURE KEY FEATURES:

- green roof
- grey water collection and use
- focus on sustainability
- minimal impact on environment
- local materials with a look towards use of traditional materials and construction methods

KAOHSIUNG STADIUM, Kaohsiung, Taiwan, 2007–9, Toyo Ito, architect.

With thousands of solar panels covering the roof, this stadium strives to support its own energy needs. It is anticipated that when not in use, it will generate enough power to support a large percentage of the surrounding area. It also has systems of rainwater collection, as well as a wind or breeze management system to keep spectators cool during summer.

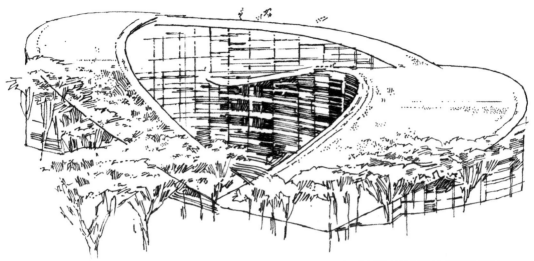

NANYANG TECHNOLOGICAL UNIVERSITY SCHOOL OF ART, Design and Media, Singapore, 2007, CPG Consultants, architects.

With an encompassing green roof that slopes and tapers in multiple directions, this five-storey structure blurs the lines between building and landscape. The roof insulates the building, harvests rainwater, cools the air and creates communal open space.

BOSCO VERTICALE, Milan, Italy, 2009–14, Stefano Boeri Architetti, architects.

The building is noted for its sustainable features of water collection and solar energy production, as well as the 18,000 growing specimens of trees, shrubs, perennials and groundcover that dominate the facade. The vegetation is intended to attract birds and insects, as well as absorb carbon dioxide and help mitigate temperature variations within the building.

BIOMORPHISM
TWENTIETH CENTURY ONWARDS

Biomorphic architecture directly references systems and patterns of biological organisms related to animals, the human body and vegetation. It strives for a visual harmony often found in nature and uses these systemic organizing principles to design architectural form.

BIOMORPHISM KEY FEATURES:

- uses systems and patterns found in nature
- mimics movement of nature
- visual harmony

QUADRACCI PAVILION, Milwaukee Art Museum, Milwaukee, Wisconsin, US, 1997–2001, Santiago Calatrava, architect.

The wings of the museum – the Burke Brise Soleil – create a moving sunscreen that opens and closes depending on the shading needs of the structure below. It has a 66-m (217-ft) wingspan and can open or close in three and a half minutes, providing a dramatic building constantly in flight.

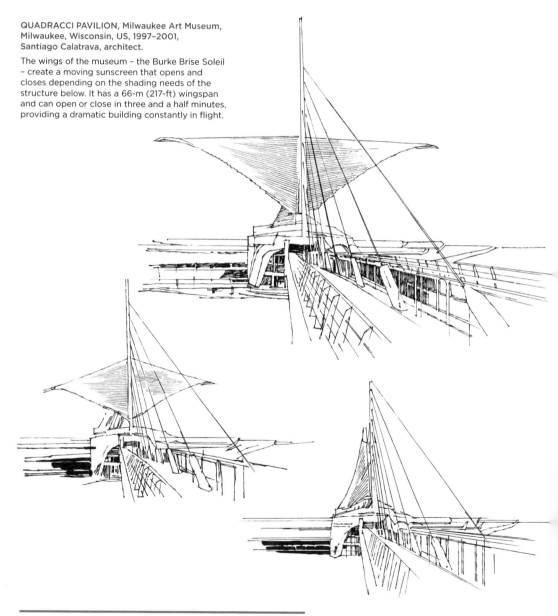

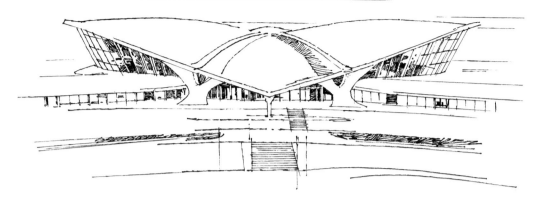

TWA FLIGHT CENTER, now TWA Hotel, Queens, New York, US, 1962, Eero Saarinen, architect.

An early example of thin-shell construction, this terminal was designed with a reinforced concrete shell that is supported at the corners as the load transfers to the ground. The project has obvious visual references to flight, with a large wing-shaped roof that lifts at each edge, providing panoramic views of planes coming and going.

LOTUS TEMPLE, New Delhi, India, 1980–86, Fariborz Sahba, architect.

This Bahā ī mashriq – temple for the Bahā ī faith – is organized around a nine-sided construction honouring the religion's belief in the powerful properties of the number nine. The temple is formed from twenty-seven marble petals grouped in sets of three to form the nine sides. At the apex of the blossom, a glass and steel aperture allows light to bathe the interior.

PARAMETRIC
TWENTIETH CENTURY ONWARDS

Parametric design relies on the iterative capacity of digital scripting programs to generate architectural space and form. Parametric is a mathematical term and references the idea that certain variables can be manipulated to modify the end result. The parametric design process in architecture is fluid, exploratory and innovative, and allows for quick formal manipulations with the adjustment of variables of input data.

PARAMETRIC KEY FEATURES:

- uses computational methods to resolve complex geometries
- digital modelling provides precise information for builders

HERTA AND PAUL AMIR BUILDING, Tel Aviv Museum of Art, Tel Aviv, Israel, 2007–11, Preston Scott Cohen, architect.

Built on a challenging triangular site, the building's surfaces twist in hyperbolic parabolas resolving the geometry of the site to the rectilinear nature of the interior spaces. The galleries are organized around the 'Lightfall', a multistorey pivoting atrium of light.

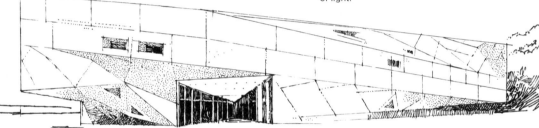

MOUNT FUJI WORLD HERITAGE CENTRE, Fujinomiya, Japan, 2017, Shigeru Ban, architect.

Shaped like an inverted mountain, the main Exhibition Building, standing five storeys tall, reflects in the pool in front of the building while Mount Fuji rises up in the distance. The curved slope woven of lattice that creates the inverted mass is made from cypress from Mount Fuji. This form extends both inside and outside the glass-framed building, while patrons move in and out and up and down its structure to circulate through the exhibits and fifth-floor viewing terrace.

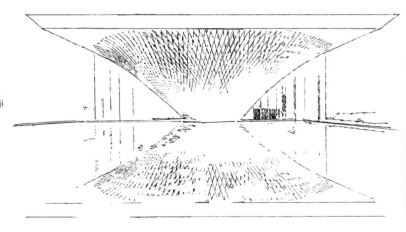

THE BROAD, Los Angeles, California, US, 2015, Diller Scofidio + Renfro, architects.

The design for this museum has two primary symbiotic volumes: the foundation volume of parking garage, and the upper volume housing art storage, offices and archives. Wrapped in a perforated facade, this 'veil' cloaks the entire building, creating a gallery space on the upper level and lifting slightly at street level to provide entrance to the museum.

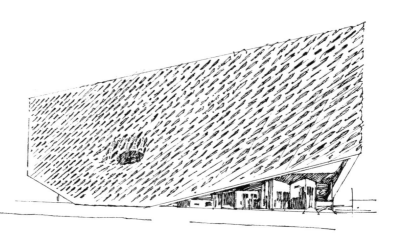

SMITHSONIAN NATIONAL MUSEUM OF AFRICAN AMERICAN HISTORY AND CULTURE, Washington, DC, US, 2012–16, Adjaye Associates, The Freelon Group, Davis Brody Bond and SmithGroup, architects.

The building is of tripartite form, sitting in direct relationship to the Washington Monument and opening to the Mall with a welcoming porch, important in its civic role as well as its references to vernacular architecture of Africa and the American South. It is wrapped entirely in an elaborate screen that serves to mitigate the sun and heat gain, referencing African artisans through its bronze material, as well as the history of African American slaves who created detailed bronze balustrades and screens found in Charleston and New Orleans.

HEYDAR ALIYEV CENTRE, Baku, Azerbaijan, 2007–12, Zaha Hadid Architects, architects.

Though amorphous in form, this cultural centre is a highly engineered and structured solution. Two primary systems work together to achieve large interior spaces free from columns: a concrete structure in conjunction with a space frame system. The cladding – fibreglass-reinforced concrete and fibreglass-reinforced polyester – allows the required plasticity of the surface.

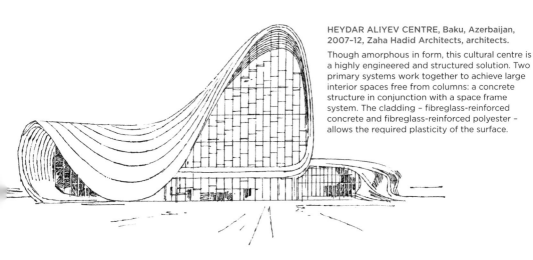

5

ELEMENTS

DOMES

The dome is technically evolved from the arch and typically used to span spaces, creating a feeling of grandeur. Structurally, a dome exerts forces both laterally and vertically, and requires a significant amount of structural technology to manage. A variety of techniques were developed to mitigate the thrust, and greatly changed the quality of space beneath and around the dome as advances were made to divert the structural load to smaller and smaller elements.

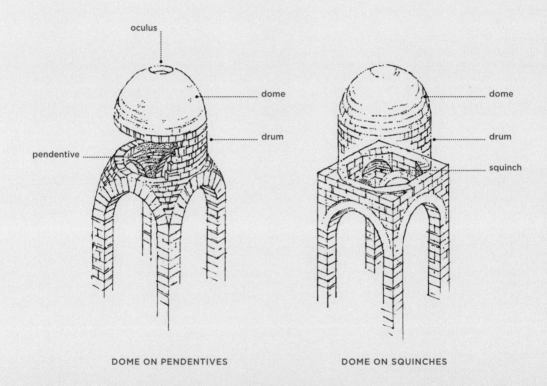

DOME ON PENDENTIVES

DOME ON SQUINCHES

Pendentives and squinches are two structural support systems designed to distribute the load of a dome with a circular base, and transfer it to a square base. Both are ancient inventions, developed in the Middle East and Ancient Rome during the late fourth and fifth centuries, and can be found in Byzantine and Islamic architecture.

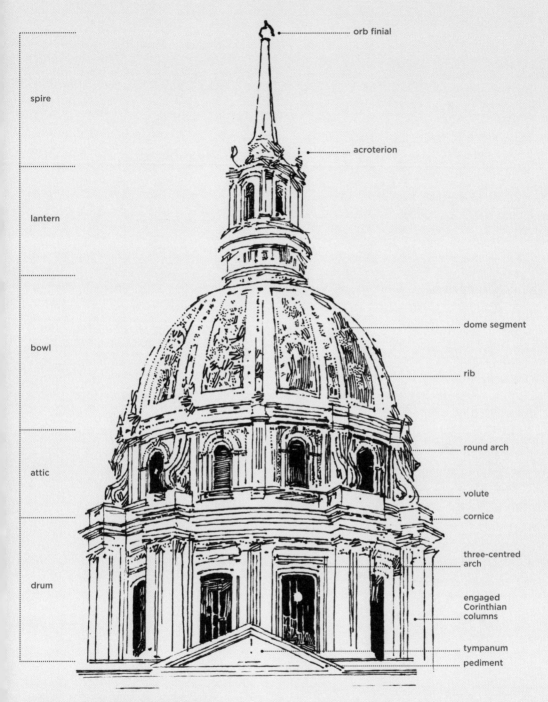

spire

lantern

bowl

attic

drum

orb finial

acroterion

dome segment

rib

round arch

volute

cornice

three-centred arch

engaged Corinthian columns

tympanum

pediment

The addition of an attic above the cornice of the drum raises the exterior profile of this dome, making it more visible from the ground at various locations around the Hôtel National des Invalides compound of a museum, church, hospital, retirement home and mausoleum in Paris, France.

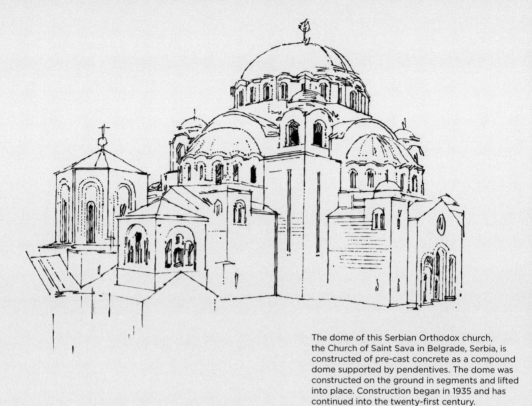

The dome of this Serbian Orthodox church, the Church of Saint Sava in Belgrade, Serbia, is constructed of pre-cast concrete as a compound dome supported by pendentives. The dome was constructed on the ground in segments and lifted into place. Construction began in 1935 and has continued into the twenty-first century.

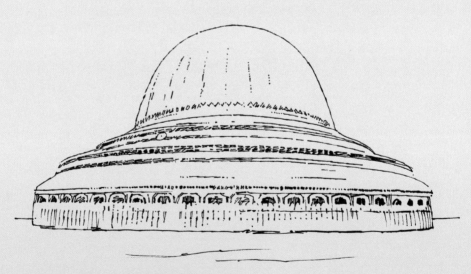

The hemispherical dome of the Kaunghmudaw Pagoda in Sagaing, Myanmar, is unusual as most Burmese pagodas are of the pyramidal style. Built in the mid-seventeenth century, it was designed and modelled after domed stupas typically found in Sri Lanka.

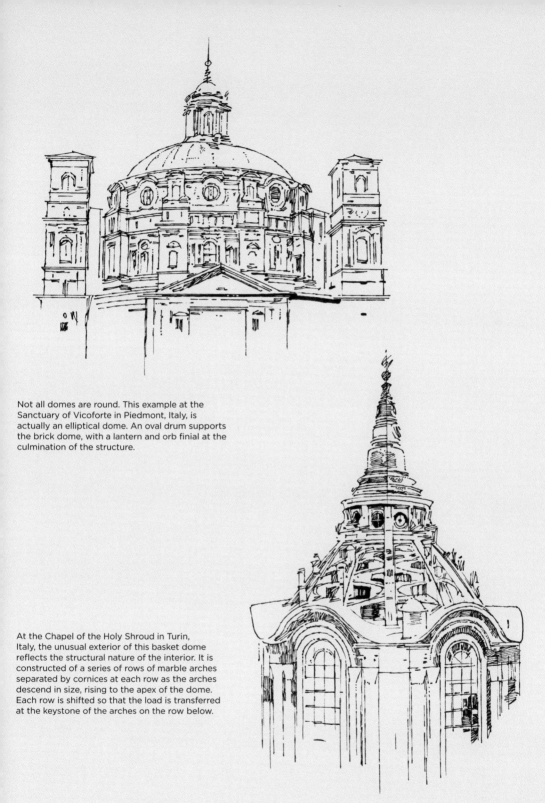

Not all domes are round. This example at the Sanctuary of Vicoforte in Piedmont, Italy, is actually an elliptical dome. An oval drum supports the brick dome, with a lantern and orb finial at the culmination of the structure.

At the Chapel of the Holy Shroud in Turin, Italy, the unusual exterior of this basket dome reflects the structural nature of the interior. It is constructed of a series of rows of marble arches separated by cornices at each row as the arches descend in size, rising to the apex of the dome. Each row is shifted so that the load is transferred at the keystone of the arches on the row below.

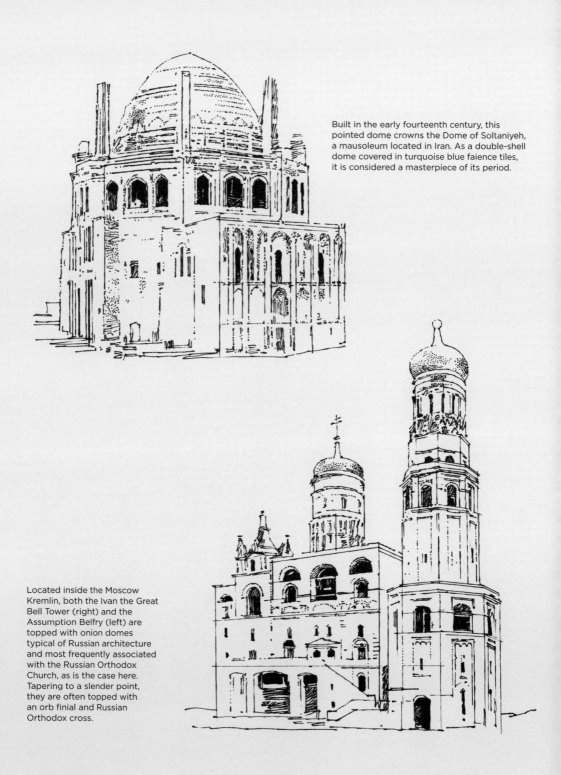

Built in the early fourteenth century, this pointed dome crowns the Dome of Soltaniyeh, a mausoleum located in Iran. As a double-shell dome covered in turquoise blue faience tiles, it is considered a masterpiece of its period.

Located inside the Moscow Kremlin, both the Ivan the Great Bell Tower (right) and the Assumption Belfry (left) are topped with onion domes typical of Russian architecture and most frequently associated with the Russian Orthodox Church, as is the case here. Tapering to a slender point, they are often topped with an orb finial and Russian Orthodox cross.

The stilted dome of the Mosque of Sultan al-Mu'ayyad in Cairo, Egypt, extends the height of the dome by vertically stretching the base. A stilted dome is similar to a stilted arch: the curve begins well above the impost line or the springer line at the base of the arch.

COLUMNS

Columns were originally developed as structural elements,
designed to carry architectural loads and to open up
architectural structures no longer reliant on solid walls.
There are five Classical orders: Tuscan, Doric, Ionic, Corinthian
and Composite. Doric, Ionic and Corinthian were originally
developed by the Greeks, whereas Tuscan and Composite were
added by the Romans. During the Renaissance, a substantial
effort was put forth to officially name, catalogue and implement
these orders with exactitude. While the Greeks used columns
purely for structure, with the development of the arch Romans
began to use these orders decoratively, which spawned new
typologies such as engaged or clustered columns.

Pairs of Corinthian columns with fluted shafts line
this grand colonnade at the Sanssouci Palace in
Potsdam, Germany. The colonnade is topped with
a deep cornice, balustraded parapet and statuary.

TUSCAN DORIC IONIC

CORINTHIAN COMPOSITE

The five Classical orders are easily distinguishable
by the column capital, which ranges from a simple
Tuscan capital to a very elaborate Composite
capital. The proportion and height of the column
shaft and base also varies for each order.
Entablatures, and all of their inherent elements –
cornice, frieze and architrave – shift in intricacies
and proportions between the five orders.

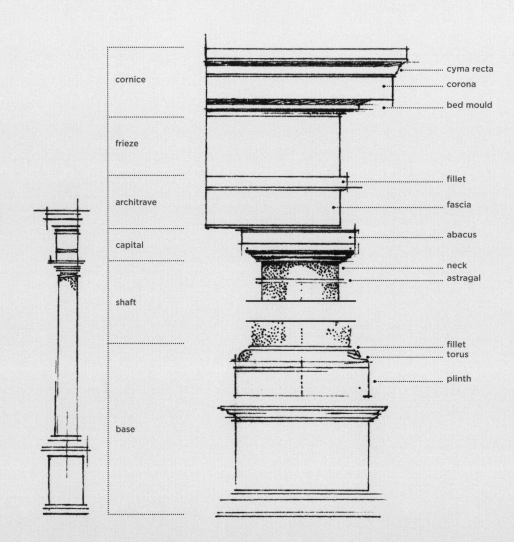

cornice

frieze

architrave

capital

shaft

base

cyma recta

corona

bed mould

fillet

fascia

abacus

neck

astragal

fillet

torus

plinth

The Tuscan order was developed by the Romans and is very similar to the Doric order in its simplicity, but closer to the Ionic order in its systems of proportion.

DORIC

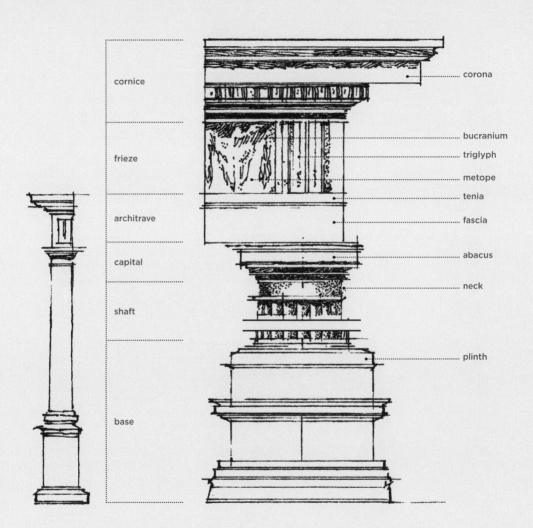

cornice

frieze

architrave

capital

shaft

base

corona

bucranium

triglyph

metope

tenia

fascia

abacus

neck

plinth

The Doric order is considered the simplest of the Greek orders, characterized by a simple round capital. This example is a Roman Doric column, which can be distinguished from Greek Doric through the addition of several elements of ornament, including the bucranium within the frieze.

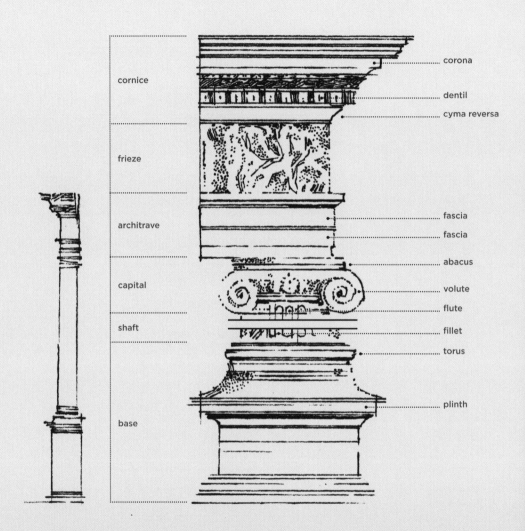

cornice

frieze

architrave

capital

shaft

base

corona

dentil

cyma reversa

fascia

fascia

abacus

volute

flute

fillet

torus

plinth

The Ionic order was established by the Greeks and is characterized by large volutes at each edge of the capital. Typically, an Ionic column is combined with a fluted shaft of twenty-four flutes, though it is also possible to see the shaft without flutes. The Ionic capital renders the volutes in one plane, except for when the column is located on a corner; in this case the volutes are at a forty-five-degree angle to mitigate the change in direction.

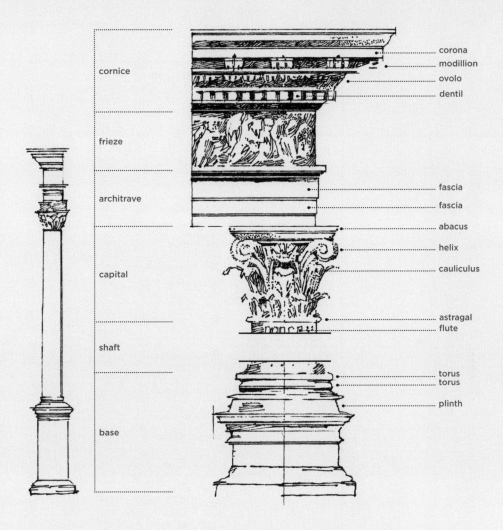

cornice

frieze

architrave

capital

shaft

base

corona
modillion
ovolo
dentil

fascia
fascia

abacus

helix

cauliculus

astragal
flute

torus
torus

plinth

The Corinthian order is the last of the orders developed by the Greeks, and is the most elaborate. The capital is a combination of helix scrolls, cauliculus stalks and acanthus leaves. The shaft of the Corinthian column is typically fluted.

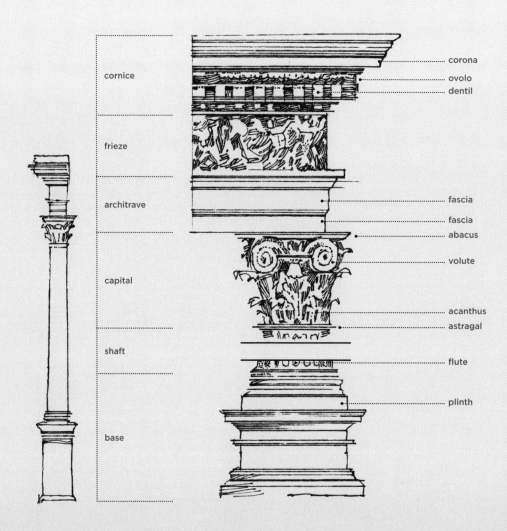

cornice

frieze

architrave

capital

shaft

base

corona

ovolo

dentil

fascia

fascia

abacus

volute

acanthus

astragal

flute

plinth

The Composite order was developed by the Romans and is considered a combination of Ionic and Corinthian. The capital is typified by large volutes of the Ionic order and acanthus leaves of the Corinthian order. The Composite order has more detail associated with it and includes ornament between the volutes. The capital is also typically much larger than in the other orders.

GREEK ERECHTHEUM
(MORE DETAIL THAN
PURE IONIC)

IONIC

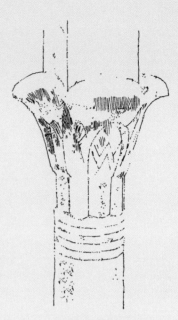

QUATREFOIL PALMETTE

CORINTHIAN

SAXON COMPOUND PIER

Column capitals are the primary means used to identify the Classical orders found in architecture. There are, however, many variations of each order that typically denote the time period in which they were fabricated or even the region in which they were fabricated. There are also many column capitals that do not fit into the Classical orders, falling outside of the Greek and Roman system, such as the palmette capital, and these unusually carved Saxon capitals from the Church of St Mary the Blessed Virgin in Sompting, England.

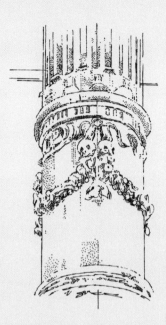

Ornate swags and fluting adorn this column.

As structural means developed, columns were often used in a more ornamental fashion, as shown with this pair.

A row of columns with their abacus or impost block engaged at the wall are topped by arches to create passage between the building wall and the column edge.

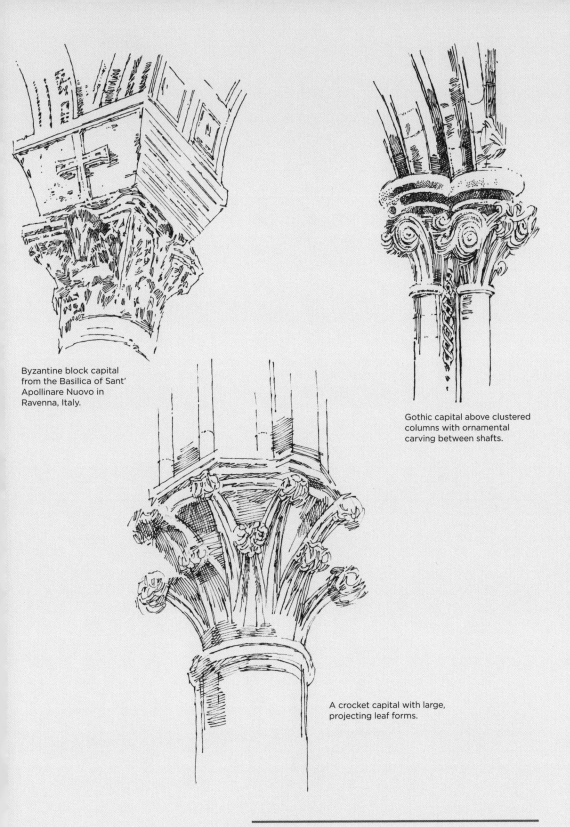

Byzantine block capital from the Basilica of Sant' Apollinare Nuovo in Ravenna, Italy.

Gothic capital above clustered columns with ornamental carving between shafts.

A crocket capital with large, projecting leaf forms.

TOWERS

By definition, towers reach above all other structures, and often perform civic as well as religious duties. They can be tall and slender or low and stout. Bell towers and clock towers operate in the civic realm to unify the community around the vertical landmark. Minarets and other religious towers are visual indicators of the significance of religion to communities. Defensive towers reinforce fortified castles, walls and other protective structures.

Islamic minarets, used to project the Muslim call to prayer, define the profile of the El-Tabia Mosque in Aswan, Egypt.

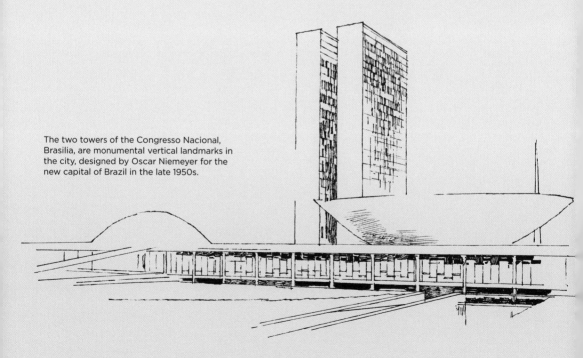

The two towers of the Congresso Nacional, Brasilia, are monumental vertical landmarks in the city, designed by Oscar Niemeyer for the new capital of Brazil in the late 1950s.

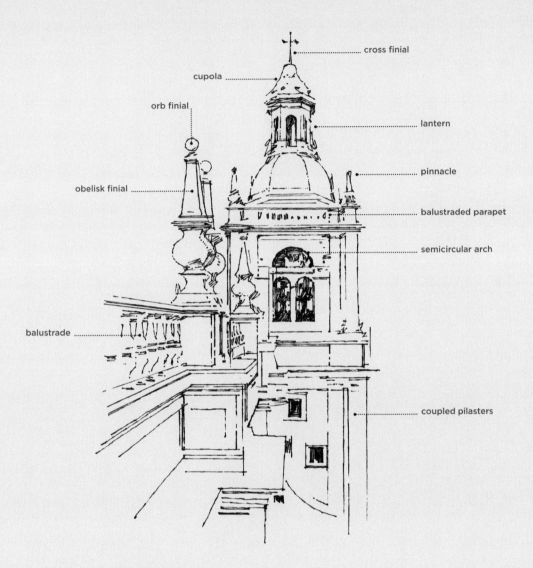

cross finial

cupola

orb finial

lantern

obelisk finial

pinnacle

balustraded parapet

semicircular arch

balustrade

coupled pilasters

Here, the tower of the Monastery of São Vicente de Fora in Lisbon, Portugal, has a small dome, lantern and cupola topping the square shaft of the tower; pinnacles mark each corner at the transition line.

The profile of this tower at
Holy Trinity Church in Leeds,
England, is defined as a
diminishing stepped tower.
It is both a bell tower and
a clock tower – each one a
significant civic necessity.

This Italian campanile – a
freestanding bell tower – acts
as a landmark of St Mark's
Square in Venice, Italy.

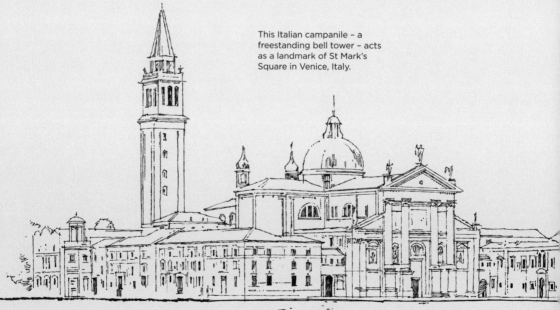

Crenellations define the
top edge of the round tower
of Nenagh Castle in Ireland,
a good example of a
Norman keep.

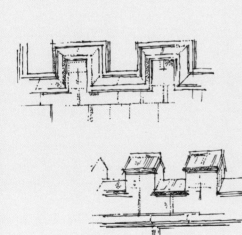

Two examples of Medieval battlements, found
along the top wall of defensive or fortified
structures. The pattern of openings provides
locations from which to launch weapons, and
places for hiding from incoming attacks.

A typical Gothic tower with a thin, tall spire
and finial projections. Triple Gothic windows in
narrow proportions amplify the soaring nature
of the tower.

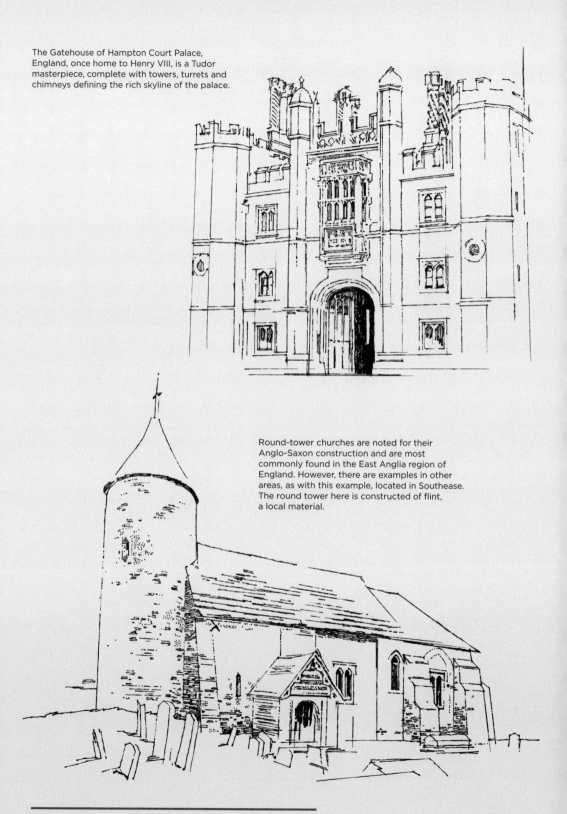

The Gatehouse of Hampton Court Palace, England, once home to Henry VIII, is a Tudor masterpiece, complete with towers, turrets and chimneys defining the rich skyline of the palace.

Round-tower churches are noted for their Anglo-Saxon construction and are most commonly found in the East Anglia region of England. However, there are examples in other areas, as with this example, located in Southease. The round tower here is constructed of flint, a local material.

The height of the towers of Neuschwanstein Castle in Germany is amplified as the entire castle is perched high above neighbouring areas, creating an overwhelming and powerful presence.

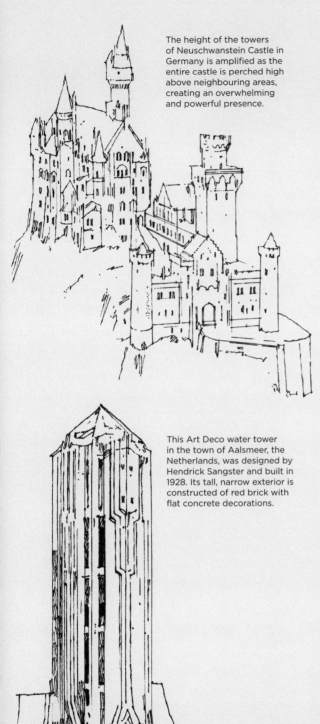

This Art Deco water tower in the town of Aalsmeer, the Netherlands, was designed by Hendrick Sangster and built in 1928. Its tall, narrow exterior is constructed of red brick with flat concrete decorations.

In Bruges, Belgium, the belfry tower stands as the predominant landmark of the city centre. This Medieval tower originally had a wooden spire that burned down in 1493 and then again in 1741. Later, in 1822, an open stone parapet was added to the top in the Gothic Revival style.

ARCHES AND ARCADES

Arches are open elements that create a span and form an opening.
Structural arches are designed to distribute the load evenly
to both sides of the span and increase in strength when a
compressive load is added. Arches can be freestanding or blind:
blind arches are applied to the surface of a wall with no openings
in between; a row of freestanding arches forms an arcade. The
arches are supported on columns or piers and typically form
an entrance or covered walkway. Arches can also be used as
decorative elements to embellish surfaces and openings.

The main entrance to the Barcelona Cathedral,
Spain, is surrounded by a deep compound arch
in the Gothic style. A compound arch is formed
through a series of stepped arches resting one
upon another in a diminishing fashion.

voussoirs

keystone

extrados

springer

intrados

SEMICIRCULAR

tympanum

impost

SEMICIRCULAR

hood mould

spandrel

TUDOR

OGEE ARCH

TUDOR ARCH

MULTIFOIL ARCH

SEGMENTED ARCH

FLAT ARCH

RELIEVING ARCH

PARABOLIC ARCH

TREFOIL ARCH

BASKET ARCH

A cut stone entrance arch to the ancient city of Ayla, now ruins, located in the modern city of Aqaba, Jordan.

Romanesque windows are often framed with round arches sitting in pairs, though other configurations are possible and still fit within the style.

The large wall with multiple rows of arched openings forms the backdrop for this ancient amphitheatre constructed at the base of the Acropolis, Odeon of Herodes Atticus, Athens, Greece in 161 CE.

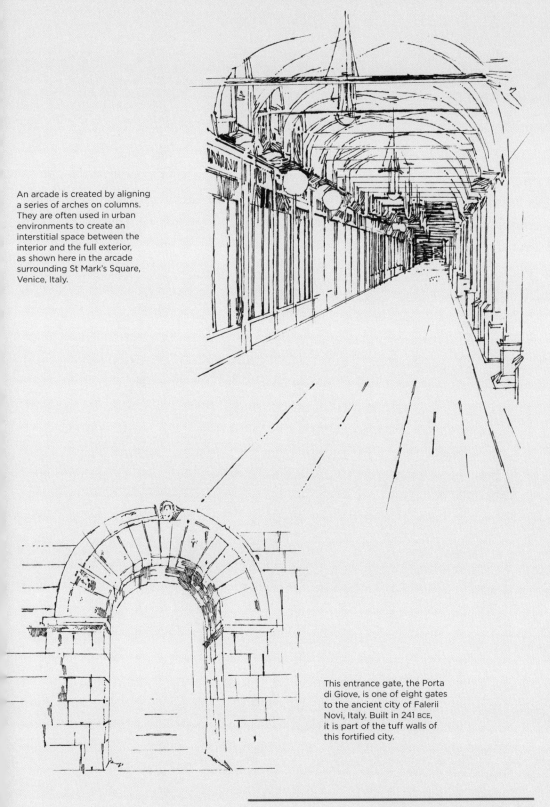

An arcade is created by aligning a series of arches on columns. They are often used in urban environments to create an interstitial space between the interior and the full exterior, as shown here in the arcade surrounding St Mark's Square, Venice, Italy.

This entrance gate, the Porta di Giove, is one of eight gates to the ancient city of Falerii Novi, Italy. Built in 241 BCE, it is part of the tuff walls of this fortified city.

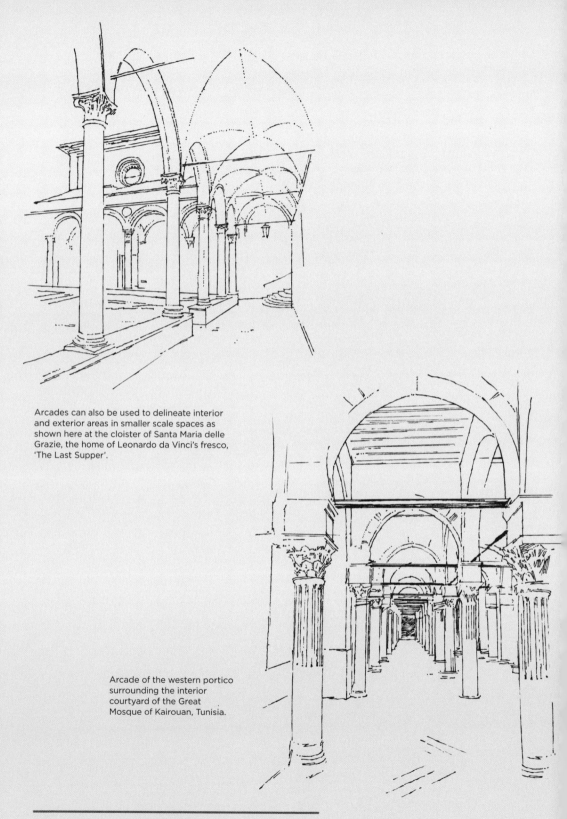

Arcades can also be used to delineate interior and exterior areas in smaller scale spaces as shown here at the cloister of Santa Maria delle Grazie, the home of Leonardo da Vinci's fresco, 'The Last Supper'.

Arcade of the western portico surrounding the interior courtyard of the Great Mosque of Kairouan, Tunisia.

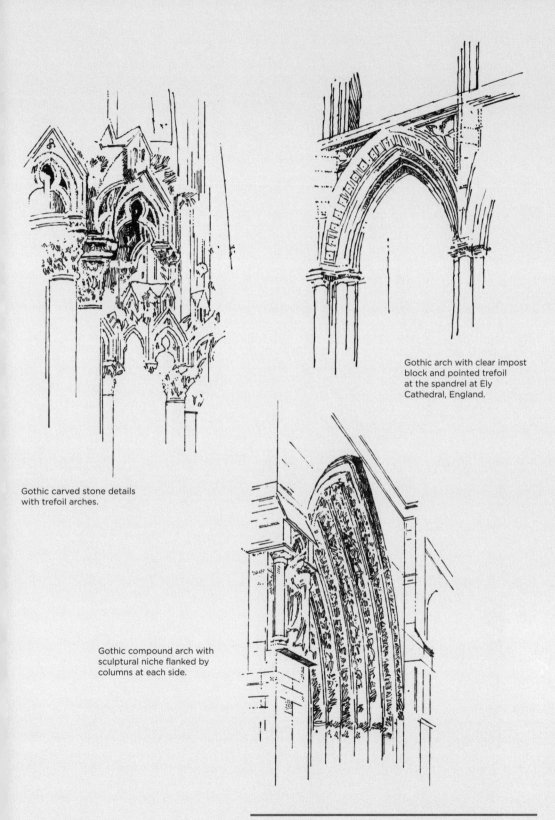

Gothic carved stone details
with trefoil arches.

Gothic arch with clear impost
block and pointed trefoil
at the spandrel at Ely
Cathedral, England.

Gothic compound arch with
sculptural niche flanked by
columns at each side.

DOORWAYS AND ENTRANCES

Doorways and entrances are an integral part of an architectural experience and provide the transition threshold between the exterior and interior of a structure. They are the place where the human body directly touches the building and where entry is permitted to the interior sanctum. This designed threshold can range in scale from the short transition of a simple door to an elongated procession of a spatial entrance sequence. The doorway is typically expressive of the style of the building and gives clues at the entry to the organization of the spaces within.

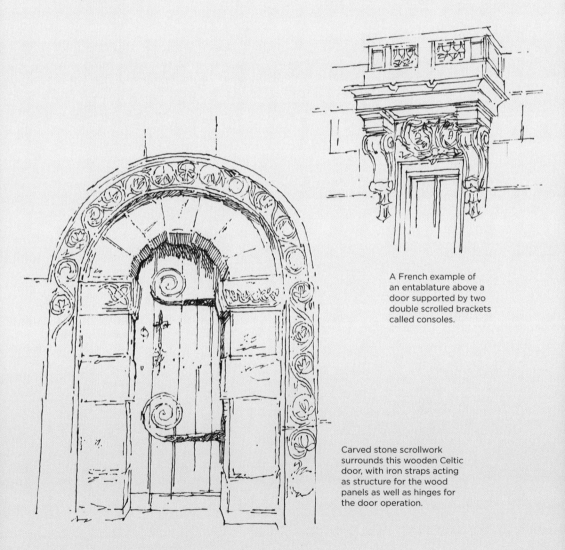

A French example of an entablature above a door supported by two double scrolled brackets called consoles.

Carved stone scrollwork surrounds this wooden Celtic door, with iron straps acting as structure for the wood panels as well as hinges for the door operation.

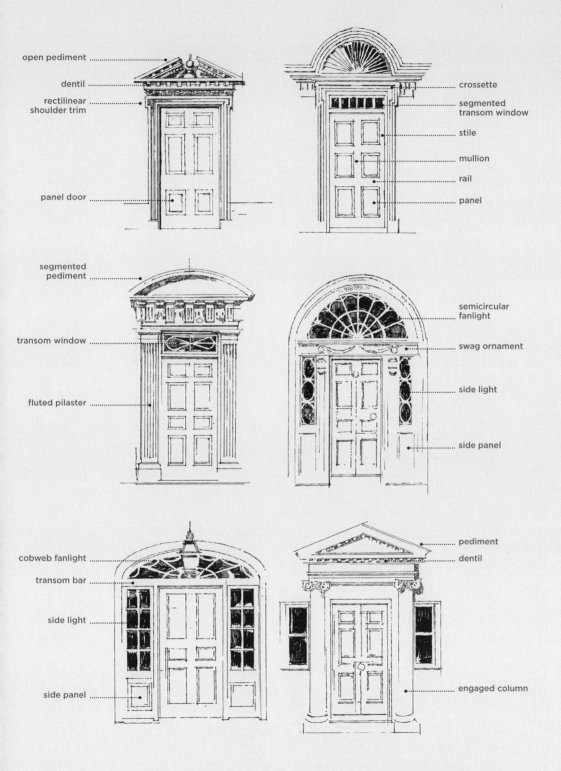

open pediment

dentil

rectilinear
shoulder trim

panel door

crossette

segmented
transom window

stile

mullion

rail

panel

segmented
pediment

transom window

fluted pilaster

semicircular
fanlight

swag ornament

side light

side panel

cobweb fanlight

transom bar

side light

side panel

pediment

dentil

engaged column

A Georgian door along
Fournier Street in London,
England. The transom window
above the door allows light
into the interior.

This wooden door in the Gothic
style has elaborate iron strapwork
on the door with a pronounced stone
surround with carved spandrels.

The keystone of the arch of this monumental
entrance to the Esken Family House Museum
in Torun, Poland, is actually a carving of a head
– an agraffe – and relates visually to the figural
carvings in the spandrel and entablature above
the door.

The American brownstone entrance elevates the home above the pavement, raising the primary floor higher than street level and providing enough ceiling clearance for an entrance to the basement level. As part of a series of terraced houses, the elevated entrances were originally designed to protect the homes from the detritus of the street.

A typical Moroccan keyhole door with double metal-panelled door and elaborately carved hood surround.

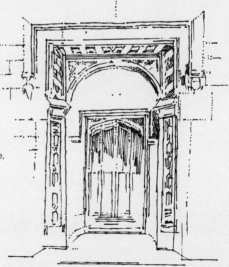

The Perpendicular Gothic style, occurring at the end of the Gothic period, is dominated by vertical elements in both tracery and panelling, as demonstrated here.

WINDOWS

Windows serve two primary purposes: to let light and air in and allow for views out. Thinking of them as apertures, simple openings in a wall, can help understand them through their function rather than their construction method or style. Recognizing windows in this way can make better sense of the different design approaches conceived to allow light and air in and views out. Originally, windows held no glass and were just openings in walls. With the advent of glass from the Romans, new possibilities emerged. Today, advances in structure, materials and systems continue to enhance the possibilities and impacts of windows in the spaces we occupy.

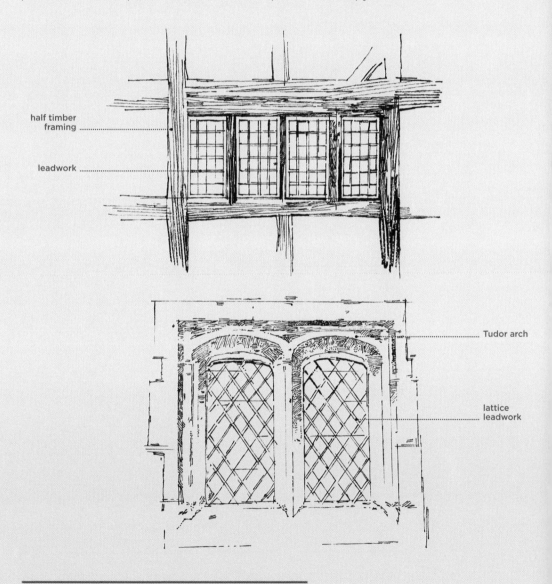

half timber framing

leadwork

Tudor arch

lattice leadwork

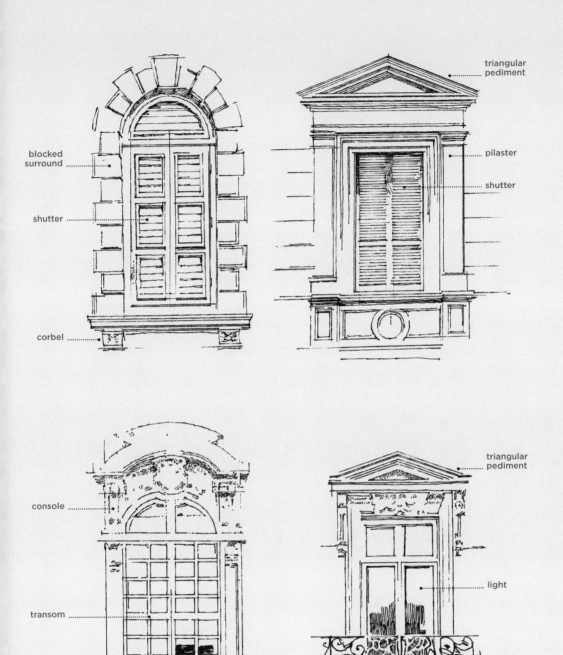

blocked
surround

shutter

corbel

triangular
pediment

pilaster

shutter

console

transom

triangular
pediment

light

balconet

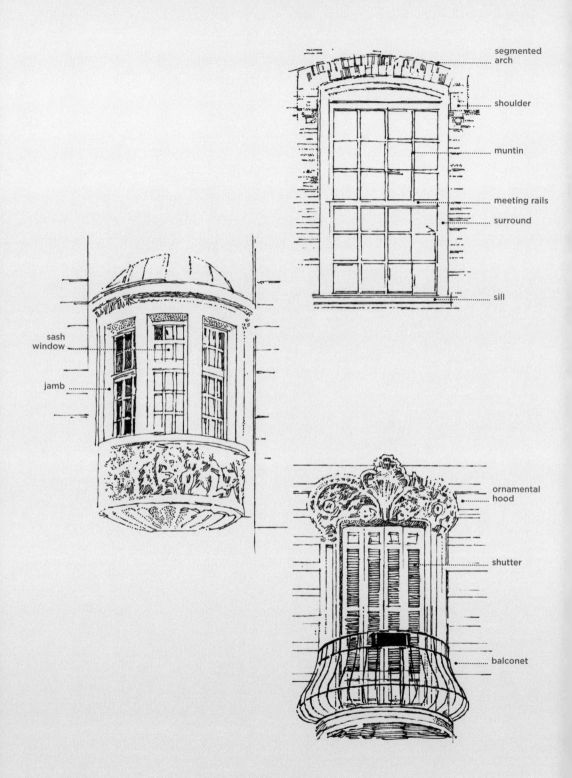

segmented arch

shoulder

muntin

meeting rails

surround

sill

sash window

jamb

ornamental hood

shutter

balconet

broken pediment ....

cornice ....

pilaster ....

light ....

This dormer window is a characteristic example of the roof window typology and projects vertically beyond the sloped plane of the roof. They are typically added to upper attic spaces to increase the head height and bring light into the space.

A rooftop squint window barely lifts off the plane of the roof to provide a small view out.

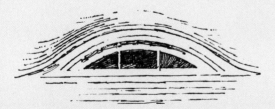

Another form of roof window is an eyebrow window that lifts up the roof plane into a curved form, letting light into an attic space.

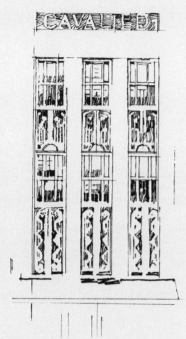

An Art Deco window from the Cavalier Hotel in Miami, Florida, US, showing ornate panelled detailing between rows of windows.

Geometric Art Deco detailing frames this fixed window flanking the entrance to the Princess Court building in London, England.

Following closely to his Five Points of Architecture, Le Corbusier referred to this house, the Villa Savoye, located just outside of Paris, France, as a 'machine for living'. Elevated on thin pilotis, it appears to hover above the ground plane. The modernist ribbon windows wrapping the entire house emphasize the horizontal nature of the design while capitalizing on the surrounding views.

This Gothic window is fitted with a label mould, also known as a rectangular hood mould, to frame the opening above the glazing.

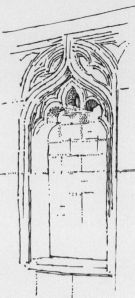

A multifoil Gothic window. Used as an ornamental device in architecture, a foil is an abstraction of a symmetrical leaf.

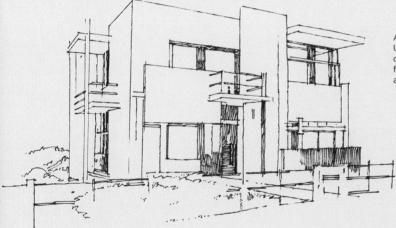

The Schröder House by Gerrit Rietveld, located in Utrecht, the Netherlands, is a quintessential example of the De Stijl movement. Along with the movement essentials – open floor plan with clear horizontal and vertical elements – the house's windows are designed to blur the line between the interior and the exterior of the structure, visually opening it further.

An ornate screened window from Vietnam.

Floor-to-ceiling steel-framed glass encloses the living areas of this Modernist Glass House by Philip Johnson in Connecticut, US. Each piece of glass is 5.5 m (18 ft) wide and framed by black steel piers and H-beams.

This example is a gable-end casement window from the High Victorian Queen Anne-style Carson Mansion in Eureka, California, US.

This carved window from Furong Ancient Town in Hunan, China, plays off its own internal symmetry and inscribes a circle within the square frame.

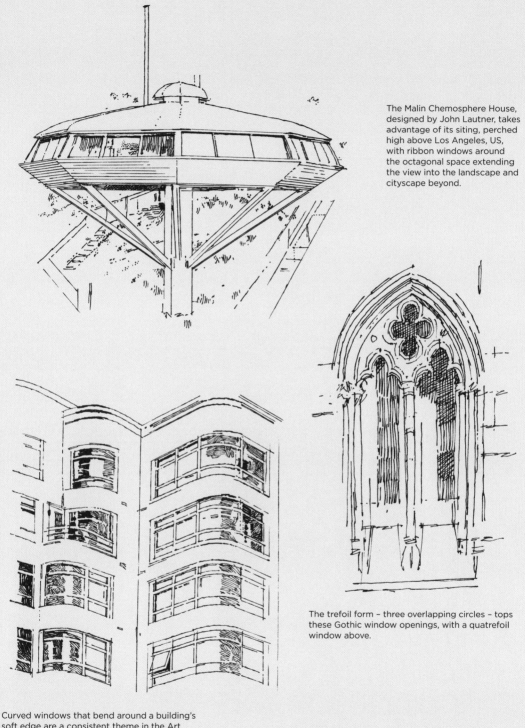

The Malin Chemosphere House, designed by John Lautner, takes advantage of its siting, perched high above Los Angeles, US, with ribbon windows around the octagonal space extending the view into the landscape and cityscape beyond.

The trefoil form – three overlapping circles – tops these Gothic window openings, with a quatrefoil window above.

Curved windows that bend around a building's soft edge are a consistent theme in the Art Deco movement.

This typical High Gothic facade boasts a central
rose window and multiple window examples
framed with bar tracery. Bar tracery is created
from thin stone mullions and replaced the visually
and structurally thicker form called plate tracery.

A canted bay window, as shown here in a typical American brownstone terraced house, extends the space and view of the main floor of the residence beyond the primary facade.

This circle bay window wraps the round room, forming the base of this turret in The Pink Lady, Eureka, California, US.

PEDIMENTS AND GABLES

The pediment, in its truest sense, originated in Classical Greek architecture and is the triangular form resting above a horizontal lintel supported on columns. A similar form, the gable, is typically the triangular wall formed from the intersection of two roof pitches. However, a gable can also extend above, and essentially hide, the line of the intersecting roofs, creating a gable parapet, as is evident in Dutch and Cape Dutch gable forms.

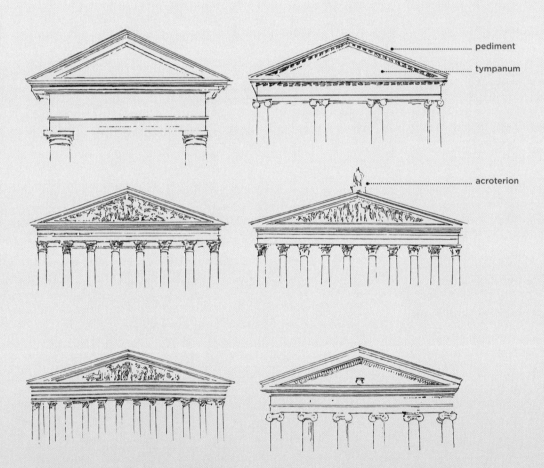

pediment

tympanum

acroterion

The proportion of a pediment, the relationship between its height and its width, has been studied extensively. While proportional relationships have been established, they vary depending on time period, construction method and column order. Ancient Greeks first developed the system and it has been continuously adapted and advanced over time.

DORIC ORDER   IONIC ORDER   CORINTHIAN
ORDER

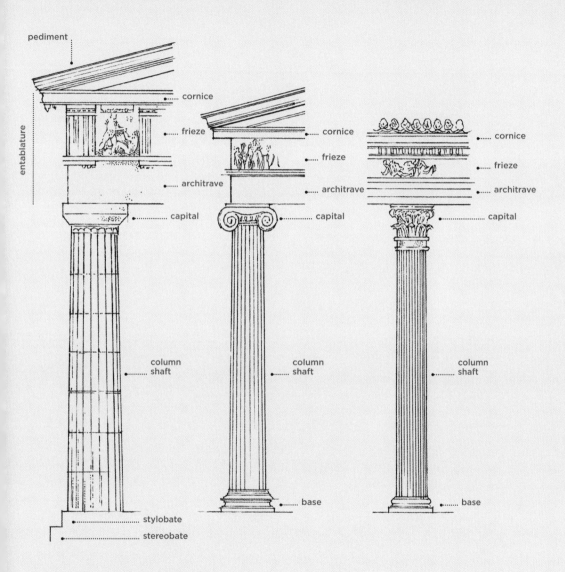

pediment

cornice

frieze

architrave

capital

entablature

cornice

frieze

architrave

capital

cornice

frieze

architrave

capital

column
shaft

column
shaft

column
shaft

base

base

stylobate

stereobate

These three orders – Doric, Ionic and Corinthian –
were developed by Ancient Greek architects and
are governed by a distinct system of proportions,
silhouettes and details. For the Greeks, columns
were developed primarily as a structural element.
Later, as the Romans developed the arch, columns
(and pediments) took on the roles of both
structure and ornament.

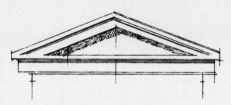

TRIANGULAR PEDIMENT

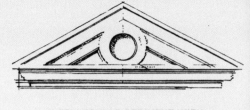

TRIANGULAR PEDIMENT WITH
INSET ROUNDEL

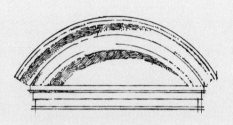

ROUNDED PEDIMENT WITH
PRONOUNCED CORNICE

BROKEN PEDIMENT

INTERSECTING PEDIMENT

INVERTED SWAN NECK PEDIMENT

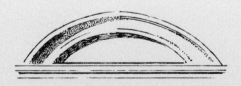

SEGMENTED PEDIMENT

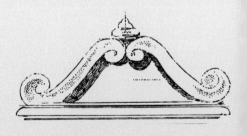

SWAN NECK PEDIMENT

Pediments can also be used at a smaller scale over windows and doors. There are endless variations that have been designed to suit the visual aesthetic requirements of different design periods.

RECEDING APEX SEGMENTED PEDIMENT

BROKEN TRIANGULAR PEDIMENT

TRIANGULAR PEDIMENT WITH
RECEDING BASE

SEGMENTED PEDIMENT WITH
RECEDING BASE

BROKEN SEGMENTED PEDIMENT WITH
RECEDING BASE

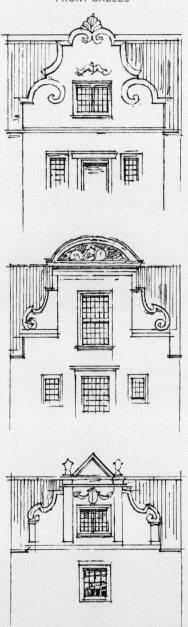
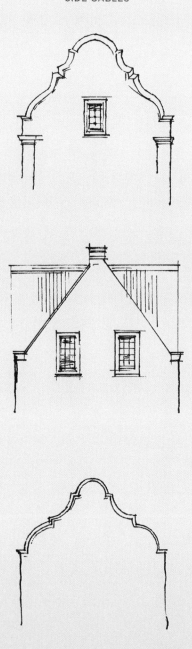

Cape Dutch architecture features both elaborate front gables and simplified side gables, as seen above. The style is found in the Western Cape of South Africa and is heavily influenced by the original Dutch settlers to the area.

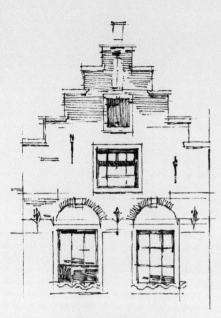

STEPPED GABLE

CONVEX GABLE

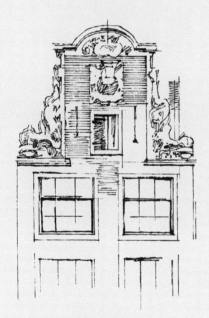

NECK GABLE

BAROQUE GABLE

Dutch gables are typically shaped at the sides and extend vertically beyond the pitch of the sloped roof to a top point above the roof line. There is often a small pediment or ornament at the apex of the gable.

ROOFS

The primary function of a roof is to provide shelter from the elements. Roofs come in a variety of forms and structural systems that reflect the region, period or style they are serving, and can provide purely functional roles, such as moving water efficiently, upholding the weight of snow or providing shade. But they also serve many aesthetic purposes, such as indicating a building's role as a civic or religious landmark, or its ecological intent. Typical shapes include pitched, flat, dome, hipped, gabled, shed, mansard, ogee, gambrel, barrel and butterfly, however many contemporary roof forms fall outside of these categories.

A shed roof can vary in slope but is characterized by one continuous pitch with no fold or bend in the roof plane, as shown in this example of a gentle shed roof pitch at Lodgepole Retreat in Colorado, US, by architects Arch 11.

Straight-line gables with no roof overhang can make it appear as though the roof material is extending down the structure to become the wall cladding.

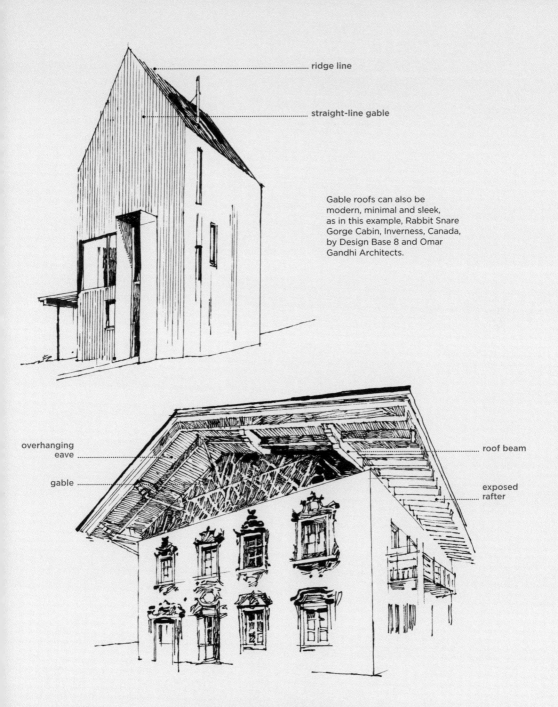

ridge line

straight-line gable

Gable roofs can also be modern, minimal and sleek, as in this example, Rabbit Snare Gorge Cabin, Inverness, Canada, by Design Base 8 and Omar Gandhi Architects.

overhanging eave

roof beam

gable

exposed rafter

The deep overhang of a traditional Bavarian home, such as this one in Garmisch-Partenkirchen, Germany, is designed to manage the extreme snow load of a typical winter in this region.

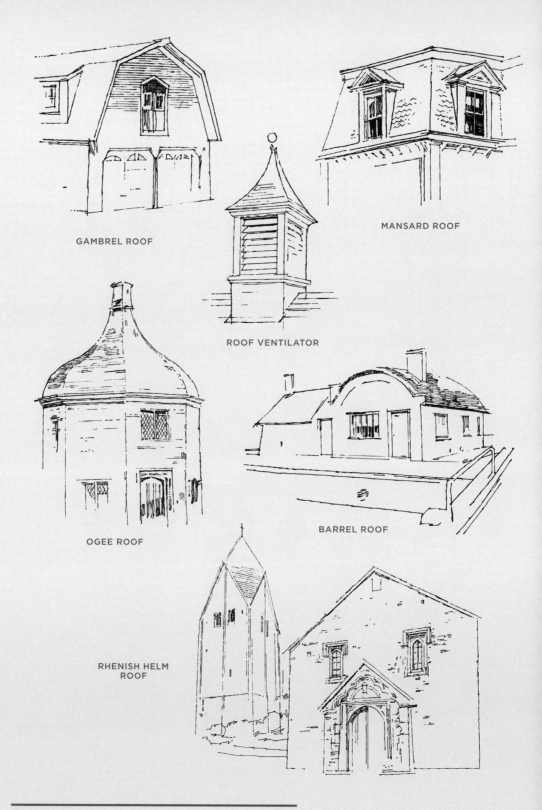

GAMBREL ROOF

MANSARD ROOF

ROOF VENTILATOR

OGEE ROOF

BARREL ROOF

RHENISH HELM
ROOF

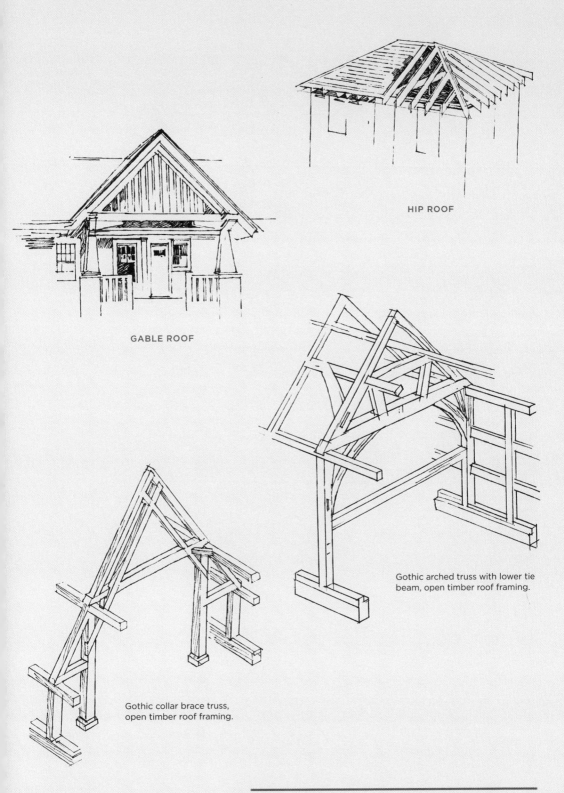

HIP ROOF

GABLE ROOF

Gothic arched truss with lower tie beam, open timber roof framing.

Gothic collar brace truss, open timber roof framing.

Round lanterns hang from the eaves of the upturned roof of this Buddhist temple in China, while ridge beasts adorn the ridge lines.

Typical Gothic heavy timber framing detail showing the arched brace between a horizontal hammer beam and vertical wall post.

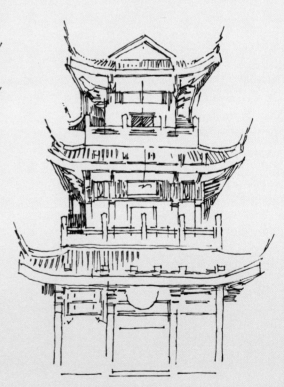

A typical Chinese upturned flying eave roof.

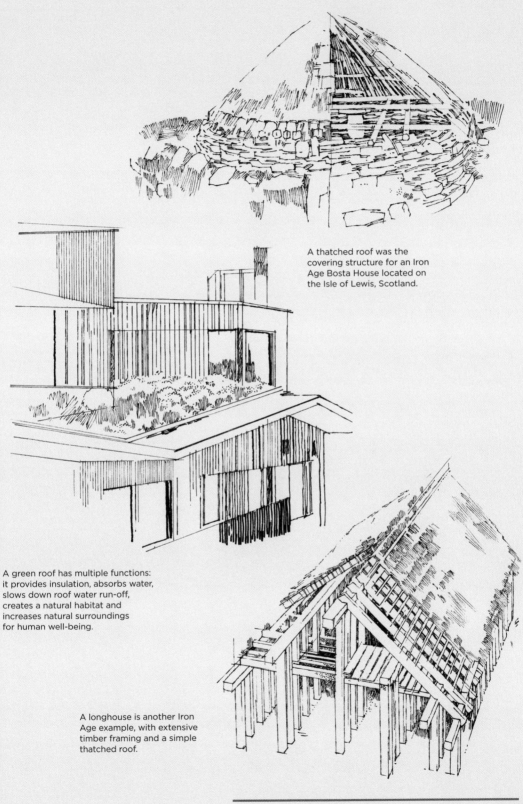

A thatched roof was the covering structure for an Iron Age Bosta House located on the Isle of Lewis, Scotland.

A green roof has multiple functions: it provides insulation, absorbs water, slows down roof water run-off, creates a natural habitat and increases natural surroundings for human well-being.

A longhouse is another Iron Age example, with extensive timber framing and a simple thatched roof.

VAULTING

Vaulting refers to a continual curved span bridging an open space. A system in use since pre-Roman times, vaulting has developed in complexity as structural methods advanced. The simplest form is the barrel vault, followed by a groin vault, rib vault and fan vault. All are designed to transfer the structural load down to a supporting system of walls, columns or piers, but must also contend with a horizontal thrust. This thrust can be mitigated in multiple ways; the most visible is through the use of flying buttresses.

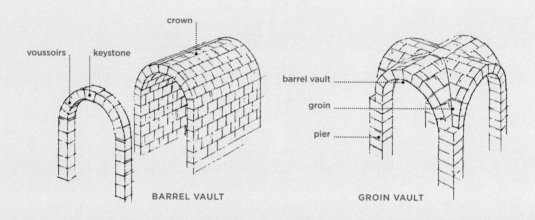

crown

voussoirs   keystone

BARREL VAULT

barrel vault

groin

pier

GROIN VAULT

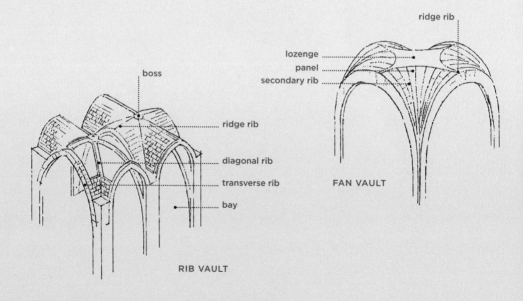

boss

ridge rib

diagonal rib

transverse rib

bay

RIB VAULT

ridge rib

lozenge

panel

secondary rib

FAN VAULT

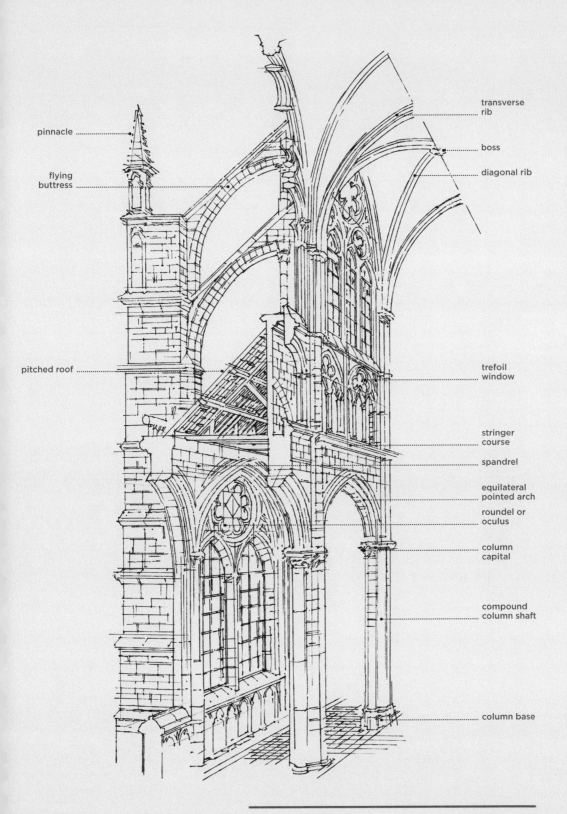

pinnacle ....

flying
buttress ....

pitched roof ....

transverse
rib

boss

diagonal rib

trefoil
window

stringer
course

spandrel

equilateral
pointed arch

roundel or
oculus

column
capital

compound
column shaft

column base

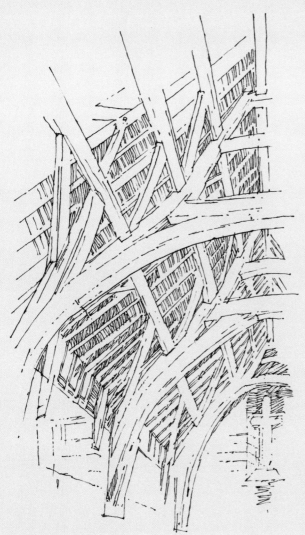

A groin vault is technically an intersection of two barrel vaults where the thrust, or load, is concentrated and distributed along the groin. This example is from the upper-level loggia of the Basilica Palladiana in Vicenza, Italy, by Palladio.

This Medieval tithe barn's wooden vaults are built in a raised crook style, with the large timbers supported on stone walls instead of reaching all the way to the ground.

This groin vault is from a vaulted chamber of the Crac des Chevaliers in Syria, a well-preserved Medieval castle from the eleventh and twelfth centuries.

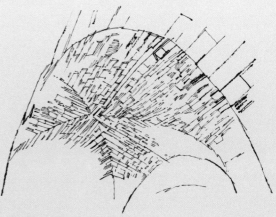

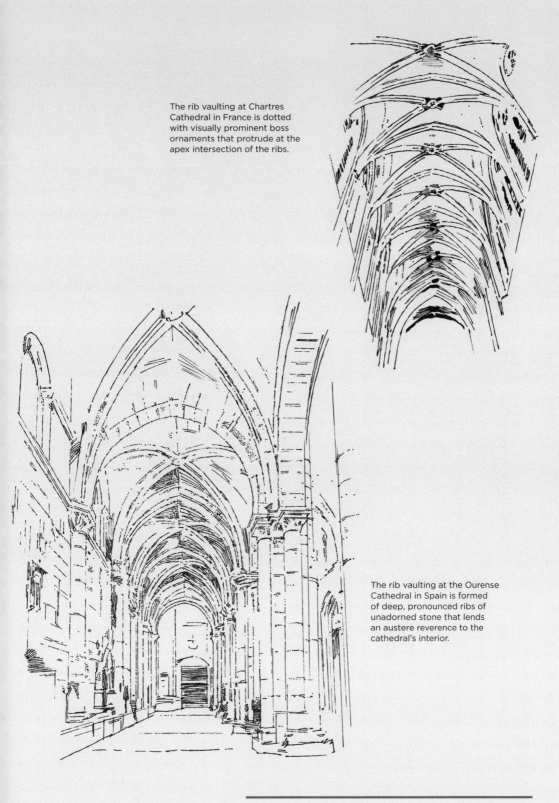

The rib vaulting at Chartres Cathedral in France is dotted with visually prominent boss ornaments that protrude at the apex intersection of the ribs.

The rib vaulting at the Ourense Cathedral in Spain is formed of deep, pronounced ribs of unadorned stone that lends an austere reverence to the cathedral's interior.

STAIRWAYS

Stairways come in an almost endless variety of forms, from simple spiral stairs to grand, monumental stairways, with varying aesthetic, processional and functional differences. Yet they all serve the exact same purpose: to move people between floors of a building or levels within a landscape. Fundamentally, the principal elements of a stairway have not changed over time, however architectural style and advances in material and structural knowledge, as well as advances in building code and safety, have greatly shifted the visual nature of stairs.

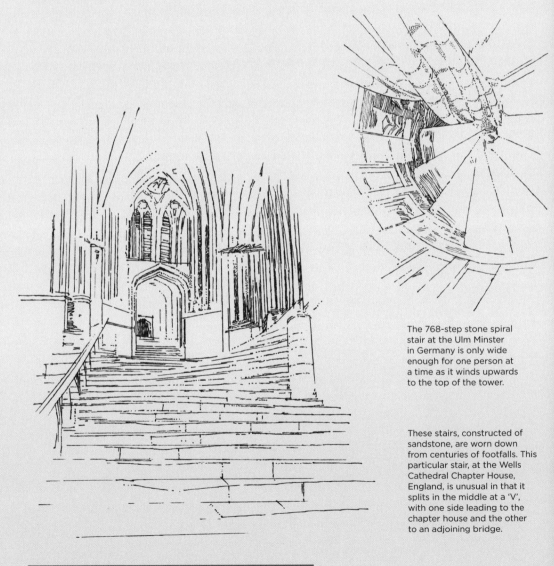

The 768-step stone spiral stair at the Ulm Minster in Germany is only wide enough for one person at a time as it winds upwards to the top of the tower.

These stairs, constructed of sandstone, are worn down from centuries of footfalls. This particular stair, at the Wells Cathedral Chapter House, England, is unusual in that it splits in the middle at a 'V', with one side leading to the chapter house and the other to an adjoining bridge.

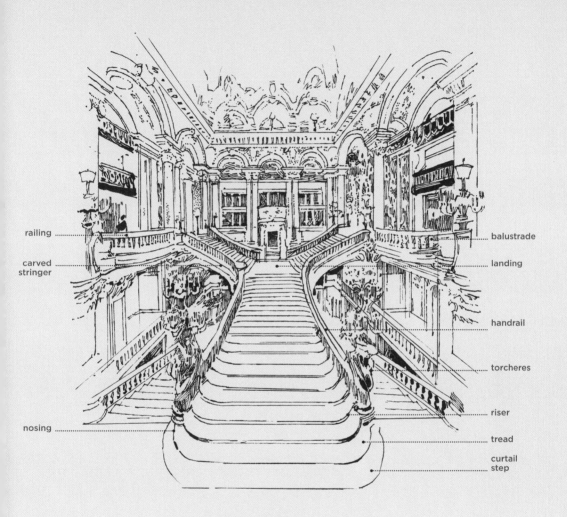

railing

carved
stringer

nosing

balustrade

landing

handrail

torcheres

riser

tread

curtail
step

The Grand Staircase at the Palais Garnier, Paris
Opera House, France, is constructed of white
marble with a red and green marble balustrade.
The stair combines a double stair, from the ground
floor, then rises into an Imperial staircase that
splits at the half landing.

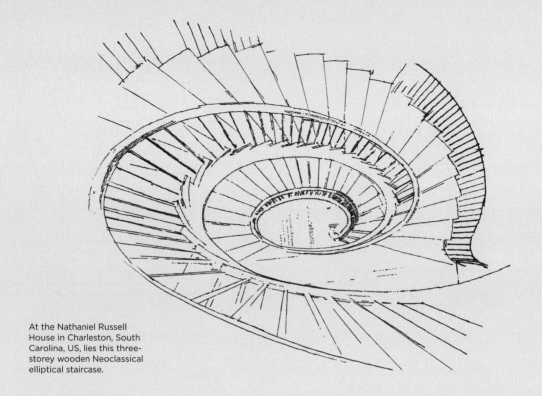

At the Nathaniel Russell
House in Charleston, South
Carolina, US, lies this three-
storey wooden Neoclassical
elliptical staircase.

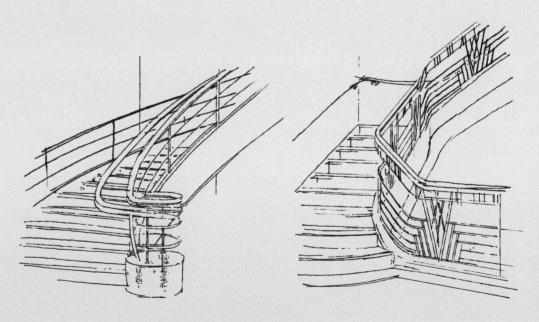

Typical Art Deco staircases have streamlined
metal handrails with geometric designs
embedded within the rail system.

An open-well staircase is described as a rectangular stair that wraps around an open well. In this case, the marble treads spill onto the floor at the base of the stair, with expanding round nosings descending to the floor.

This beautiful late-Gothic open-carved, exposed stone staircase is called the Booksellers' Staircase at the Rouen Cathedral, France. The upper flight was added when an additional floor was built above the library.

The internal stair from the Sir John Soane's Museum in London, England, is a fine example of a winding stair – a stair that turns a corner without a landing – in a traditional Georgian town house.

GLOSSARY

adytum (Greek) / adyton (Latin)
A small sanctuary or deity space located in the inner chamber of a temple, an area restricted to priests and other religious celebrants.

all'antica
A style of the Italian Renaissance, in which architects borrowed from Ancient (*antica*) Rome. However, opportunities, innovation or constraints, such as the narrow city plot awarded to Vincenzo Scamozzi (1552–1616) for his Teatro all'antica (1590), resulted in a reflective, not a copyist, style.

ambo
An early predecessor of the Christian church pulpit, comprising a small, mobile, stepped platform, often railed, on which the Gospel or Epistle was read to a congregation.

apadana
A columned audience hall particular to the Achaemenid (Persian) Empire, with open triple porticos on the north, east and west sides, monumental entrance staircases, stone columns and wooden ceiling beams.

arch
A curved, open construction, whose lateral thrust on its two sides is contained by abutments. Open arches such as bridges require inward thrust to keep the ends from spreading, with anchorage provided by either natural (riverbanks, canyons) or artificial (buttresses) sources. Used in Western and Islamic architecture, types common to both include the pointed arch. Those more specific to Islamic architecture include the horseshoe and poly-lobed arches, while those particular to the West include the lancet, trefoil and Tudor.

bad gir
A traditional Persian wind tower that 'catches' and redistributes air currents into a building. Known in Arabic as *malqaf*, the basic square tower design is used in multiple countries, but vent designs can differ regionally and nationally.

baldachin
An interior canopy placed over a secular throne or religious altar. It can be suspended, freestanding or projected from a wall.

ballcourt
A narrow, open-air playing field found in Mesoamerica, walled on its two long sides. Originally open-ended, later designs enclosed the end zones to create an L-shaped structure.

Beaux-Arts (*adj*)
An eclectic style of the late nineteenth and early twentieth centuries that borrowed and adapted the monumentality and rich decorative detail of French architecture from the sixteenth to nineteenth centuries.

berm
A raised earth barrier or earth parapet. Medieval military engineers used berms between a parapet or defensive wall and a walled ditch or moat. Contemporary use includes earth-sheltered architecture for high insulation value.

boiserie
A French term for wood panelling or wainscot (panelling on the lower part of a wall only), used primarily in reference to elaborate shallow-relief carved interior panelling of the seventeenth and eighteenth centuries.

brise-soleil
A permanent sun-break feature used to shade windows (often vertical or horizontal fins, but also including open-patterned masonry blocks), particularly in hot climates. It was popularized by Le Corbusier, but has roots in vernacular Islamic architecture.

buttress
A masonry or brickwork mass that supports a wall. Buttress types include 'clasping', which creates a flush embrace to a building angle, and 'flying', which is an arch or half-arch brace that repels the building's outward thrust. More basic buttresses include timber planks wedged at forty-five-degree angles against walls.

cella
The inner area of an Ancient Greek or Roman temple, which housed the image of the deity. Also known as the naos.

charbagh
A Persian-derived quadrilateral garden with four axial paths or water courses. The design strongly influenced Mughal garden plans.

chhatri
A dome-shaped pavilion on the roof of a building. It is commonly associated with Indian architecture, particularly the Rajput architecture of Rajasthan.

Chicago window
A three-part window composed of a fixed sash (non-opening) window in the centre, framed on either side by narrow movable sash windows. It is associated with the Chicago School of architecture of the late nineteenth and early twentieth centuries. Iterations include casement windows on either side of the fixed central window.

chinoiserie
A style of architecture imitative of Chinese models, particularly pagodas. It was popular in Europe during the seventeenth and eighteenth centuries.

ciborium
An interior canopy over a Christian altar that is supported on columns. It is similar to the baldachin.

clerestory
A windowed area in the upper part of a church nave, above the aisle roofs. Its unimpeded location enables light to infiltrate the interior. The term is also used to describe similar arrangements that are found in secular buildings and domestic architecture.

Coade stone
A fired ceramic 'stone' produced from a white pottery clay, to which is added sand, powdered flint, quartz (to vitrify) and 'grog' (waste ceramic). It was marketed in eighteenth-century England by Eleanor Coade, who called it Lithodipyra (stone fired twice). The material remained popular into the early nineteenth century for monuments, sculpture, and architectural decoration.

Cor-ten
Known generically as 'weathering steel', Cor-Ten is the trademark name of a steel alloy that forms an intentional protective rust skin. It has perceived decorative properties that differ in outcome depending on the environment, location and level of exposure to the elements.

Corinthian
A Greek architectural order. The Corinthian order developed in the fifth century BCE and went on to become the favoured style of the Romans. It is distinguished by its elaborate capital, which was carved with two staggered rows of stylized acanthus leaves and four scrolls.

crenellated
Describes a building with battlements, in particular the symmetrical, alternating vertical pattern of low points (embrasures) and high points (merlons) on the top of a parapet.

Doric
A Greek architectural order. The Doric order was established by the first quarter of the sixth century BCE and was characterized by a fluted column that rested directly on the floor of the temple without a base, topped by a plain, unadorned capital.

exedra
An outdoor bench in a semicircular or rectangular recess. It can also refer to the apse of a church or to a niche therein.

feng shui
The Chinese art of orientating and arranging objects and structures to harmonize with the spiritual forces of yin and yang, thus enabling the appropriate flow of energies.

ferro cemento
The Italian term for ferrocement, a Portland cement and sand mix with plaster-like fluidity. When placed over a reinforced-steel framework, it can be used to create structures that are light, thin and plastic. Material failure is generally limited to deformation or spider cracks. Round ferrocement water tanks are renowned for their longevity and low maintenance.

formwork
Also known as 'shuttering', formwork is a temporary or permanent timber, metal, fibreglass or plastic mould that holds and shapes poured concrete until it cures, to create precast concrete. The formwork's texture, particularly timber, will imprint on the concrete. Intentional textures and raised-profile finishes are created with bespoke formliners placed inside the mould.

gambrel
A roof with two sides, each of which has two slopes. On both sides a shallower slope sits above a steeper one.

gopura
Often one in a series, the gopura is a rectangular entrance gateway with a barrel vault roof that is found in southern Indian Hindu temple enclosures. Gopuras steadily increased in size from the mid-twelfth century to become colossal gateways dominating temple complexes.

gunite
A mixture of cement, sand and water that is sprayed through a pressure hose, producing a dense, hard layer of concrete.

High-Tech (*adj*)
A style of architecture inspired by the materials and techniques associated with engineering and other technologies. The term was adopted from the interior design book *High Tech: The Industrial Style Sourcebook for the Home* (1978) by Joan Kron and Suzanne Slesin, and replaced the 'Industrial Style' label that was used to describe such architecture in the 1970s.

Ionic
A Greek architectural order. The Ionic order originated in Ionia (today part of Turkey) during the mid-sixth century BCE, and featured a slimmer profile with a greater number of flutes on the pillar. The bottom of the column rested on a moulded base, while the capital at the top was decorated with volutes (scroll-like ornaments).

International Style
An architectural style that emphasized form over social context, as first defined by Henry Russell Hitchcock and Philip Johnson in 1932. Lasting from approximately 1925 to 1965, the style emerged from the European Modernist movement and the Bauhaus. Focus then shifted to the United States, from where the style was exported globally.

iwan
A rectangular hall or room located near the entrance of a mosque, usually vaulted with one end open. Also known as liwan, they are sometimes used in domestic Islamic architecture.

jaali
A pierced screen carved in an open calligraphic or geometric pattern, which allows air exchange and permits semi-concealed views. It is used in Islamic and Indian architecture.

jalousie windows
Also known as louvres, jalousie windows are lapped, horizontal glass or wood panels held in twin vertical tracks, which allow the plates to open outwards in unison via a mechanical crank handle or central wooden rod. They are common to semi-tropical and tropical climates and are often paired with external shutters. The plates can be angled to allow them to be open during rainstorms without rain ingress.

keystone
A wedge-shaped stone in the apex of an arch or vault that locks the other stones in place by allowing lateral forces to 'lean' into it.

Lady Chapel
A Christian chapel dedicated to the Virgin Mary, typically built as a projecting satellite east of the high altar in a cathedral and south of the high altar in a church. It is generally rectangular in plan.

loggia
A long gallery open on one or more sides, supported by columns. The main open side is usually orientated towards a specific view, such as a public square or a garden.

mansard roof
A double-slope roof where the lower slope on each of its four sides is taller and more acutely angled than the smaller four-sided upper slope, whose lower pitch can conceal it from casual observation. The design is characteristic of the French Renaissance and was a common feature of nineteenth-century Second Empire architecture.

mashrabiya
A window or projecting enclosure shielded by intricately carved wooden latticework. An element of traditional Arabic architecture since the Middle Ages, it enables the occupants of a building to survey the outside without being seen, in addition to providing shade and natural ventilation. Highly skilled carpenters dovetailed each piece of the screen to allow for natural expansion and contraction of the wood under the duress of extreme heat.

mestizo
An eighteenth- and nineteenth-century vernacular interpretation of European Baroque architecture, found in provincial areas of Spain's colonial territories in South America. Its chief characteristic is intentional deep shadows created by undercut carving.

metopes
A square space between the triglyphs of a Doric frieze, often decorated with carved work.

muqarnas
A decorative transitional feature used in Islamic architecture, such as between a squinch arch and a dome. Corbel-like projections are intricately tiled in mathematical patterns, of which three geographically diverse core designs have currently been idenfitied.

naos
See *cella*.

narthex
A general term for the antechurch (porch) at the entrance of a Medieval Christian church. Two types of narthex are found in Byzantine churches: the esonarthex, which precedes the nave and aisles, and the exonarthex, which precedes the facade. For both types, the division is made clear by columns, rails or a wall between the zones.

oculus (*plural* oculi)
A circular opening located at the apex of a dome.

ogee arch
A pointed arch with an S-shaped curve on both sides.

opisthodomos
The room positioned at the rear of an Ancient Greek temple, furthest from the main entrance.

pendentive
A concave triangular space that acts as a transition between a circular dome and the square or polygonal base on which the dome is set.

peripteros
An Ancient Greek or Roman temple cell that is enclosed by a continuous wall, surrounded at a proportionate distance by a gallery of columns creating a portico.

piano nobile
The main floor of a grand house, containing public reception rooms. Generally it is located on a raised ground floor and has higher ceilings than the storeys above.

piloti
Pillars, columns or stilts that support the raised floor of a building, leaving open circulation beneath. Popularized by Le Corbusier, their origins lie in vernacular architecture. Variations include Oscar Niemeyer's V-shaped and W-shaped piloti.

pisé de terre
The French term for rammed (compressed) earth wall construction. An ancient and natural building method, it has high thermal efficiency and uses sustainable materials such as earth, chalk, lime or gravel.

pishtaq
A prominent projecting gateway or portal of a mosque, often an arched doorway set within a flat rectangular 'frame' that leads to the iwan. It served to emphasize a building's presence.

pronaos
An anteroom at the front of an Ancient Greek temple, forming a portico immediately in front of the cella.

porte-cochère
A covered entrance to a building that provides shelter for passengers entering and leaving carriages or cars. Generally it is open on all four sides, with a driveway running through its centre.

quadriga
A two-wheeled chariot drawn by four horses abreast.

reinforced concrete
A type of concrete in which metal bars or wire are embedded to increase its tensile strength.

Serlian window
A three-part window consisting of a central window with an arched head flanked on either side by a usually narrower window with a square head. It is named after Sebastiano Serlio, who described the design in *L'architettura* (1537). It is also known as a Palladian window, as similar openings were common in the work of Andrea Palladio.

stack ventilation
A natural form of ventilation that exploits the phenomenon of hot air rising above cool air in an enclosed space (stack effect). Providing an exit for the hot air creates a partial vacuum, which draws in cooler air from the outside atmosphere to replace the hot air in a cyclical fashion. The system works best in climates with marked differentials between exterior and interior temperatures.

stupa
A domed or beehive-shaped Buddhist commemorative monument.

synthronon
A series of clerical benches in early Christian and Byzantine churches that were placed in a semicircle in the apse or in rows on either side of the bema (a raised area in the apse).

talud-tablero
A Pre-Columbian Mesoamerican style, also known as slope-and-panel, which is commonly associated with the pyramids at Teotihuacán in Mexico. It consists of an inward-sloping wall (the talud), atop which rests a platform (the tablero) that generally protrudes slightly from the lower section.

tatami
A traditional rice straw and rush Japanese floor mat. It is made according to a standard aspect ratio of 2:1. This gave rise to the 'jo' unit of measurement for real estate area, whereby one jo corresponds to the size of one tatami mat. Measurements vary regionally and older buildings may differ in jo measurements from newer builds.

tempietto
A small, temple-like building, often circular.

tholos
Refers to the dome of a circular building; the round domed building itself; or a stone, corbel-vaulted, pointed dome Mycenean tomb.

timber framing
A carpentry-based construction method also known as post and beam, which connects large pieces of timber with woodworking joints such as the mortise and tenon (whereby a hole is made to receive a projection of similar dimension, creating a 'male–female' joint). Areas between the open wood frame are infilled with a material such as plaster, brick, wood siding or straw bale.

trabeated
A basic construction method also known as the post-and-lintel system, where two upright posts support a bridging horizontal lintel across their top surfaces.

triforium
An arcade above the arches of the nave of a church, forming an upper storey to the aisle between the nave and the clerestory.

trumeau
The central vertical post support in a trabeated doorway, often used to support a half-circle tympanum in Christian churches and cathedrals.

tympanum
The semicircular or triangular area above a doorway, bounded by a lintel and arch. It is often decorated with relief sculpture.

X-brace
An X-shaped brace that allows a building's lateral load to be reduced by transferring it to the exterior. It was developed by engineer Fazlur Khan. His application of a hinged flexible X-frame stiffened with diagonal supports to the exterior of the John Hancock Center (1970) in Chicago revolutionized skyscrapers in terms of achievable heights and reductions in the total weight of steel required.

zenana
The zoned quarters, apartments or areas that are reserved for women in Islamic architecture. They can range from elaborately designed rooms in royal complexes to simple screened or curtained areas.

INDEX

Margaret Fletcher was educated at Harvard University Graduate School of Design and is an Associate Professor of Architecture, the Associate Chair of the Architecture Program and holds the Ann and Batey Gresham Professorship at Auburn University. Through her design collaboration at Mack Scogin Merrill Elam Architects, Fletcher has participated in projects that have won over 12 American Institute of Architects (AIA) Awards including three National Awards of Excellence. She was named one of the 30 Most Admired Architectural Educators in the United States by DesignIntelligence for 2019–20.

Robbie Polley is an architectural illustrator with more than 25 years' experience. Trained at the Royal College of Art, London, he has since worked on major architecture projects in the UK and internationally – from the New British Library to the Lisbon Expo. Equally at home working in pencil, ink, watercolour and Photoshop, his drawings have featured in 30 books, including many DK Eyewitness travel guides and *Architecture Inside + Out* (Thames & Hudson, 2018).

First published in the United Kingdom in 2021 by
Thames & Hudson Ltd, 181A High Holborn,
London WC1V 7QX

Reprinted in 2023

Conceived, edited and designed by
Quintessence, an imprint of The Quarto Group
The Old Brewery
6 Blundell Street
London N7 9BH

www.quartoknows.com

Editor: Emma Harverson
Designer: Hugh Schermuly
Art director: Gemma Wilson
Publisher: Samantha Warrington

British Library Cataloguing-in-Publication Data
A catalogue record for this book is available from
the British Library

ISBN 978-0-500-34364-7

Printed in Malaysia

MIX
Paper | Supporting
responsible forestry
FSC® C007207
www.fsc.org

Be the first to know about our new releases,
exclusive content and author events by visiting
thamesandhudson.com
thamesandhudsonusa.com
thamesandhudson.com.au

FLATIRON BUILDING, New York City, New York, US